THE ENGLISH PRISON HULKS

H.M.S. York as a hulk at Portsmouth, 1828

THE
ENGLISH
PRISON HULKS

by

W. BRANCH-JOHNSON

With a Foreword by

HUGH J. KLARE

(Secretary, The Howard League for Penal Reform)

CHRISTOPHER JOHNSON

LONDON

CHRISTOPHER JONNSON © 1957

First published 1957

SET IN 12 ON 13 PT. GARAMOND AND PRINTED AND MADE
IN GREAT BRITAIN BY PAGE BROS. (NORWICH) LTD. FOR
CHRISTOPHER JOHNSON PUBLISHERS LTD.,
11/14 STANHOPE MEWS WEST, LONDON, S.W.7

CONTENTS

[v]

To
The Memory of
My Old Friend
Philip Macer-Wright

LIST OF ILLUSTRATIONS

Except where otherwise indicated, illustrations are from ILLUSTRATED LONDON NEWS—to which paper acknowledgements and thanks are due.

FOREWORD

THOUGH a great deal has been written on English prisons, their administration and their history, Mr. Branch-Johnson's book on prison hulks is the first of its kind. Through much of it, he has allowed facts and historical documents to speak for themselves; and neither pull any punches. The treatment of convicts in prison hulks was abominable and remained so for a long time, despite the efforts of John Howard and other reformers. Apathy, complacency, the realisation of the sheer effort and imagination required to interfere in the self-perpetuating impetus of an existing system, and to bring about an effective change in direction—these were the things that stood in the way of a more enlightened and humane approach to treatment of prisoners.

To some extent, they still do. The nineteenth century answer to prison hulks was the erection of specially built, permanent jails. Alas, they proved to be only too permanent. Pentonville and its grim brood, meant to serve a system of punitive repression, strict separation, silence, and the discipline of the treadmill, still house the majority of our prisoners, and no one has yet succeeded in providing a full day's work of a reasonably constructive kind for all those who lie in jail. Yet just because there have been great improvements in penal methods, and the evils of the present system are much less obvious than those of the days of the prison hulks, public apathy and complacency are perhaps harder to combat than ever before.

I commend this book to all. Some will feel justifiable satisfaction at the progress made in the treatment of offenders since the days of "transports in suspense", as prison hulks have been described. Others will reflect somewhat wryly that at least a few of the observations made in this book are still applicable today. Amongst these others, I find myself—in company, I suspect, with the author.

HUGH J. KLARE

1957

Chapter One

A TEMPORARY EXPEDIENT

NEARLY everybody has heard of the English prison
hulks. Yet this book is their first detailed story. For
a variety of reasons, writers on penal methods have
not troubled much about them; to the rest of us they tend
to rank with the galleys as vaguely apprehended chambers
of horror not too closely confined to any particular period of
history.

The brief truth is that, having been established rather less
than two centuries ago, they remained in use as floating
prisons for civil prisoners into the lifetime of a few people
still with us, and survive vestigially at the present day.
During the Palestine troubles which followed the Second
World War, an immigrant vessel was forced to detain her
human cargo on board, unconvicted prisoners, for several
months at Haifa. From 1922 to 1925 the Government
of Northern Ireland lodged its political opponents on board
the *Argenta* in Belfast Lough; and during the First World
War, in 1915, nine liners were moored in the Thames off
Southend for Germans awaiting repatriation. In short, the
principle, so to speak, of prison hulks is, even to-day, not
quite dead.

What justification has that principle to survive?

[1]

Elizabeth I's Act for the Punishment of Rogues, Vaga-
bonds and Sturdy Beggars, in 1597, enforced transportation
as the sentence next in severity to death, and no toll is
now possible of those—not always felons, but sometimes
vagrants, or men and women illegally impressed—who
were carried across the Atlantic to Virginia, Jamaica,
Barbados, and other "plantations", where cheap labour was
constantly in demand. Political and religious prisoners too
were frequent transports; to ship them half over the globe
and into virtual slavery was a convenient way of ridding the
country of their sedition and turbulence. Judge Jeffreys
utilised transportation freely and, at a later date, the failure
of the Forty Five condemned many of its participants to
gruelling toil in the New World.

A special government office, known as the Transport
Office, operated the system, while a competitive industry
outside Government control grew up about the carrying
and settling of felons overseas. The attitude of these
contractors, as they were called, appears to us callous in the
seventeenth century and no less callous in the eighteenth;
but, as men of their time, they provoked little qualm among
their contemporaries. Nevertheless, thanks to John Howard
and his followers, notions of "reforming" both the criminal
and his prison surroundings were beginning to crystallise
in religious and parliamentary minds, when a complete
breakdown of the transportation system was precipitated
by the revolt of the American colonies in 1775. With two
hundred capital offences on the Statute Book, some com-
mutable to transportation, and an equally large number
for which transportation was the normal punishment,
Justices throughout the kingdom continued to sentence
those who appeared before them to seven, fourteen or
twenty-one years overseas, until the gaols were filled, and
more than filled, with waiting transports for whom no

destination could be provided. Parliament, suddenly alive to the situation, was at its wits' end.

It solved the problem by inaugurating what it termed, and no doubt believed to be, a "temporary expedient". Since, it declared, transportation to America "is found to be attended with various inconveniences, particularly by depriving this Kingdom of many subjects whose labour might be useful to the community", any male "lawfully convicted of great or petty larceny, or any other crime for which he shall be liable by law to a sentence of transportation to any of His Majesty's colonies or plantations in America . . . shall be punished by being kept to hard labour in the raising of sand, soil and gravel, and cleansing the river Thames, or any other service for the benefit of the navigation of the said river". This Act, which was supported by Burke, Lord North, Sir Frederick Eden and other prominent members of the House, and which, indeed, received little opposition from any quarter, was limited in its operation to one year; but, periodically renewed and extended in scope "for the more severe and effectual punishment of atrocious and daring offenders", it helped to give birth to a new idea in English penal methods—the idea of hard labour at home.

Supervision of the prisoners thus employed was left to the Justices of Middlesex. They appointed, as they had been ordered to do, an Overseer, Duncan Campbell, to take charge of the work ashore. As deputy he named his brother, Neil Campbell. The appointment made, and an assurance received that he would lodge no financial claim with them, they sat back and gave their attention to presumably weightier matters. During the next twenty years not a single minute on this subject appears in the Quarter Sessions Records of the county.

Now the Act provided not only for an Overseer but also

for a contractor to supply food, shelter and clothing to the Thames-side convicts. Campbell was appointed to this post also—with the result that the convicts were delivered completely into his hands. For at least six years a transportation contractor (he described himself as a merchant), who had in that period carried many hundreds of felons in chains across the Atlantic, he knew his business. He provided a ship of his own, the *Justitia*, 260 tons, purchased an old frigate, the *Censor*, from the Admiralty, dismantled them, built a pent-house or two on their decks, anchored them in the stream of the river between Gallions Reach and Barking Reach and decanted into them as many prisoners as they would hold, brought thither from all parts of the country, chained two and two by the leg. The Act received royal assent at the end of May 1776; by August the temporary expedient was in full swing.

The condition of the bed and foreshore of the Thames was notoriously bad at this period; the work of cleansing it was therefore regarded as of immense public benefit. It soon became known, moreover, that convicts were converting the shelving banks of the Warren, as it was called, into docks, quays and yards for the Royal Arsenal at Woolwich. Before many months, popular interest had been captured, and convicts at work became recognised as among the sights of the Capital. Indeed, so frequent and so large became sightseeing parties that steps had to be taken to prevent them from approaching too close. Says a newspaper of the period: "The place where the convicts are now at work is enclosed on the land side by a brick wall, so that spectators will soon (if not already) be barred the sight of these miserable wretches on the land side, except at a distance".

But even though prevented from seeing "these miserable wretches" at labour, the public could still read about them. A typical "account of the employment and treatment of the convicts presently employed in ballast-heaving on the Thames" was contributed to the *Scots Magazine* in July 1777 by "a gentleman who saw them at work".

"There are upwards of two hundred of them", he wrote, "who are employed as follows: Some are sent about a mile below Woolwich in lighters to raise ballast, and to row it back to the embankment at Woolwich Warren, close to the end of the Target walk: others are there employed in throwing it from the lighters. Some wheel it to different parts to be sifted: others wheel it from the Skreen, and spread it for the embankment. A party is continually busied in turning round a machine for driving piles to secure the embankment from the rapidity of the tides. Carpenters, etc., are employed in repairing the *Justitia* and *Toyloe* (*Censor*) hulks, that lie hard by for the nightly reception of those objects, who have fetters on each leg, with a chain between, that ties variously, some round their middle, others upright to the throat. Some are chained two and two; and others, whose crimes have been enormous, with heavy fetters. Six or seven are continually walking about with them with drawn cutlasses, to prevent their escape and likewise to prevent idleness. So far from being permitted to speak to anyone, they hardly dare speak to each other. But what is most surprising, is the revolution in manners: not an oath is to be heard; and each criminal performs the task assigned to him with industry, and without murmuring. It seems as if each convict was most desirous of showing his readiness and his obedience to discipline, being induced thereto by one only hope, viz., that of obtaining their liberty by good behaviour, which is the only means afforded them to get their liberty before the legal expiration of their time. . . . All is discretionary with their keeper. They do not take it by turns to work, but turn out of the hulk into the long boat, and go on shore to work as he pleases, without distinction. If anyone appears to keep behind, he is certain of being employed the oftener. The greatest liberty allowed them is that of being permitted to go to a neighbouring ditch within their boundaries to drink."

On the whole, a picture suggesting orderliness of design, stability of policy, and acquiescence on the part of the prisoners. Yet these first years of the hulks were in reality turbulent ones. Repeated attempts to file away or knock off the chains about the convicts' waists and ankles led to floggings galore, extra irons, imprisonment in the Black Hole. In November 1776, five men seized the arms chest on board the *Justitia*, drove the warders below, and escaped in a boat brought alongside by their friends; in the pursuit two were killed, one wounded, and two recaptured. Shortly afterwards eight attempted to imitate the exploit; then fourteen, who, having got clear away as far as Greenwich, met a naval officer and were, for the most part, persuaded by him to give themselves up. A little later, twenty-two forced their way, one Sunday afternoon, into the Captain's cabin, armed themselves with the pistols and cutlasses they found there, rowed to the north bank of the river, and, by raiding a blacksmith's shop, freed themselves of their fetters. At East Ham, however, they were overtaken by a party of sailors from the Arsenal, and a lively skirmish ensued in which one of the runaways was killed and three re-taken, the rest fleeing into Epping Forest. Some managed to make good their escape; others were re-captured by ones and twos during the next few months, and hanged.

These, however, were but preludes to a much more serious affair in September 1778. One morning the Captain of the hulks, Stewart Erskine, received an anonymous letter informing him that the lives of himself and his officers were in danger.

"The Captain, upon this warning", says the *Morning Chronicle*, "immediately went to the shore, where about 250 convicts were then at work, and cautioned his people, who were placed to guard them, to be prepared. Shortly after 4 o'clock in the afternoon, about 150 of them assembled in a body, having first armed themselves with pikes, taken from the *chevaux de frize*, with axes and spades, and proceeded to the only pass where they could effect their escape, which was firmly guarded by about 20 well-armed men. The Captain remonstrated strongly, and repeatedly endeavoured by gentle means to dissuade them from such an attempt which, if persisted in, must cost some of them their lives. This had no effect on their desperate leaders, one of whom instantly attacked and wounded the Captain, still pressing forward to the pass, throwing showers of heavy stones, and threatening to murder all who opposed them. At last the ship's people were obliged to make use of their firearms, which, with the assistance of those of a party of artillery, obliged the convicts to retire. Two of their leaders were killed on the spot, and seven or eight more were much wounded."

Yet even after such a stern lesson the convicts were not subdued. Next day thirty-six of them made a sudden rush upon the warders and succeeded in getting safely away from the hulk; no sooner were they in the stream of the river than the warders opened fire, killing one, wounding eighteen, and eventually recapturing the remainder, who were brought on board and loaded with chains, partly to prevent a repetition of the incident, partly as a warning to the rest.

How far did the conditions in which prisoners lived on board the *Justitia* and the *Censor*, off Woolwich, explain such outbreaks? When Howard first published his "State of the Prisons", in 1777, he drew firm though guarded attention to them—he forbore from entering into detail, he said, on account of the temporary nature of the experiment. But, apart from print, he was busy in remonstrance; and when the Act of 1776 came up a second time for renewal, he and his friends succeeded in inducing Parliament to appoint a Committee of Inquiry, under the chairmanship of Sir Charles Bunbury. It is true that the Committee, in recommending a new Bill "to continue the present Mode of punishing Convicts on board the Hulks by Hard Labour", reported that "the said Hulks are at present convenient, airy, and healthy"; by what strange process they arrived at that opinion—just as by what process subsequent Committees arrived at similar conclusions—becomes indeed mysterious when we consider upon what evidence it was based.

Chapter Two

CAMPBELL'S ACADEMY

"CAMPBELL'S ACADEMY" was the title playfully bestowed upon the hulks by writers in the public press; the two reports of the Committee under Sir Charles Bunbury—in 1778 and 1779—show how bitter was the title in its irony. While on shore thinking men were turning their minds to "reforming", if not the circumstances which produced criminals, at least criminals when made, the hulks from the very first were left, presumably by carelessness, outside the channel of that reforming spirit. The Act of 1776 omitted to provide for the appointment of a chaplain. During the first year, those who died were buried hugger-mugger in unconsecrated ground along the fore-shore of the river; afterwards, Campbell obtained a piece of land on the outskirts of the Arsenal and buried them there, the funeral service being performed by one of his officers.

The evidence given before the Committee came—with one exception—from those whose interest it was to present the hulks in a favourable light; it came from Campbell, from Campbell's officers, from outsiders whom Campbell had paid, from Campbell's friends. Campbell himself had several contracts with the Government—one awarded him £38 a man a year, the others averaged £27.

Out of the sums thus received he had, it is true, to provide vessels, maintain forty officers, and meet many other expenses. But, especially since the trade of transportation contracting was at a standstill, he had above everything to reap a profit for himself. No instructions had been given him as to the manner in which the ships were to be fitted out or the establishment run. Would it not be unreasonable (so he probably argued) to expect him to perfect a temporary expedient? He was a "merchant", and acted as such.

If the evidence tendered by the one witness outside the Campbell clique—John Howard—had contradicted too completely the story given by those who were more or less constantly on board the hulks, we might be compelled to discount it; admissions and mutual contradictions already made by the clique go a long way towards supporting its general tone. One of Campbell's friends, a medical man, might give it as his considered opinion that "he thought there was all possible care taken of them"—that is, of the convicts; condemnation of his regime had already come from the mouth of Campbell himself, when he told how, in two years, 176 prisoners out of a total of 632 had died—almost one in three; and in the third year a rather greater proportion. On the voyages of convict ships to the American plantations, he was forced to admit, "upon an average of seven years, the loss of convicts in gaol and on board will be one-seventh."

The first convicts put on board the hulks, in August 1776, were healthy but despondent. "Universal depression of spirits", as Campbell described it, endured; eight out of ten of the prisoners, said one of his surgeons, died from it alone, "without any fever or other disorder upon them." Another witness declared that "he had visited many of the gaols in London, but saw none so affected." In spite of the steps which Campbell took to alleviate it—notably allowing the men to labour without their irons ("but they made bad use of it"), and recommending a certain number for pardon, in order to encourage the rest—depression continued. It was reflected in their work—they performed, according to most witnesses, only about one third the task of a free labourer. It was reflected, as we have seen, in their repeated attempts to escape. It was reflected most disastrously of all in their health. Little more than two months had been passed on board, when an epidemic of gaol fever—a form of typhus spread mainly by vermin— was raging among them, and persisted with greater or less severity for more than three years. Dysentery—due, one doctor suggested, to drinking brackish water—the itch, and venereal diseases were also rampant. Campbell does not seem to have thought it necessary to appoint a medical officer at all, until it appeared possible that he might lose his contracts by the death of all his charges; when he called in an assistant-surgeon of Artillery, the epidemic had obtained a stranglehold. Whereupon the assistant-surgeon joined with other medical men who had had to be summoned in attributing the origin of the outbreaks to county gaols— Gloucester, Maidstone, Cambridge, Plymouth, and Nottingham were specially mentioned, while it was added that of "those who are sent from Newgate, 20 out of 40 have the venereal complaint". But no epidemic is known to have occurred in any of these gaols during the years they were alleged to be filling the hulks with infected prisoners.

Hospitals were nothing but the forecastles of the two vessels, where, according to Howard, "they had nailed up a few boards to separate the healthy from the sick". From them emerged "a disagreeable odour". At first, patients, whatever their complaint, lay upon the bare floor; later they were given straw mattresses, their irons were removed, and, in the words of one of the doctors, "they are kept

clean and neat". Certain indulgences were allowed them—
"rice gruel, balm tea, and a little wine if necessary", so that
"the diet of the sick cannot be amended". Yet, if the diet
was as perfect as it was said to be, even some of the doctors
could not wax enthusiastic over the accommodation.
Although one described the hospitals as "commodious",
the majority united in condemning them, not on the ground
that they were centres of infection, but merely as cramped,
and recommended either a special hospital ship or, better
still, the erection of a building on shore. But Campbell,
who admitted that when he inspected the hulks twice a
week he never went inside the hospital, was loath to embark
upon any such costly scheme.

When Howard first visited the hulks, in October 1776,
he said, "he saw all the prisoners together upon deck" and
among them one whom he perceived to be very ill. "He
touched his pulse and asked him how he did? He said, He
was ready to sink into the earth. The witness immediately
turned to his conductor, and the conductor swore an oath,
and said that the convict had the venereal disease (the
conductor was an Inspector of the convicts, one of the head
officers, as witness supposes). The witness then said, Some
care ought to be taken of this man; the conductor said,
The man had a draught yesterday; the witness then asked
the man if he had had it, and he said, No; the witness then
turned to the conductor and the conductor said nothing;
the witness found afterwards by inquiry that no care had
been taken of this man; the witness then asked the conductor
how he could tell him such a falsity, and he said nothing.
The witness saw many others who looked sickly; and he
enquired of them whether they had any medical assistance,
and they said they had no surgeon or apothecary, that
nothing had been done to save this man from that dis-
temper."

There were, in addition, other aspects of life in the hulks which were both depressing to mind and disastrous to health; one of the most potent, if subtle, to men who were supposed to be undergoing "reformation" by hard labour, was the happy-go-lucky method in which work ashore was organised. The officers who superintended it at the Arsenal, under the direction of the Board of Ordnance, were slack; Campbell, since "he derives no advantage from their labour", took only a perfunctory interest in it. "They have", said Howard, "no regular plan with regard to their working"; and his statement was grudgingly corroborated even by the contractor's friends. Campbell attributed the inefficiency of the men to the necessity of wearing irons, and to a certain extent he was right; but Howard claimed that "if it had been properly overlooked, more work might have been done". During the fine season ten hours' labour was the rule; during the winter, seven. It was, however, frequently found impossible to employ all the convicts at the same time. Those who were called upon to work in these circumstances were chosen arbitrarily, while the rest remained in idleness on board. In wet weather and on Sundays none worked; they sat about dejectedly, moped, grumbled, recounted past misdeeds to companions anxious to profit by their experience, and planned mutinies and escapes.

Not only were they irregularly employed and often idle; they were overcrowded. The *Justitia* (260 tons, it will be recalled) housed about 125 prisoners; the *Censor*, a rather larger vessel, 183—in addition, of course, to forty officers distributed between the two ships. One deck, scarcely high enough to allow a man to stand upright, had to serve for the prisoners; the officers lived in cabins in the stern. Several doctors commented, if but vaguely, on this over-crowding and its effect upon the health of already depressed convicts; they commented in much stronger language, as did Campbell himself, on the inappropriateness of some of the prisoners to their punishment. For they included—these "daring and atrocious offenders" for whom the hulks had been established—men over seventy years of age, men blind, crippled, or mad; and, during the first three years, eight boys not yet fifteen years old, and another eight not yet sixteen, who were employed in such scouring as the hulks received. Yet, though one of Campbell's friends might describe the two ships as "remarkably clean", a foul odour infested the vessels from end to end—notably, as one doctor remarked, "near the Necessary". Portholes on the river side could be opened; those to landward were blocked up, so that through ventilation was almost impossible to obtain. In one big, unencumbered space below, prisoners slept, fed, and, when not at work, lived throughout the day, except for a short period of exercise on the top deck. By Campbell's orders the *Justitia* was never washed, "as he thought the men might catch cold". Yet Campbell complained more than once, in his evidence before the Committee, that it was harder to make the men wash than to make them work. They were supposed to wash every morning—"those who are well enough", as one doctor put it—to shave once a week, and to change their shirts on Sundays; but the average man tends to rise or fall to the level of his surroundings, and a glimpse of their natural preference in matters of cleanliness is obtained from the statement that "some of them" undressed to go to bed.

The scene which greeted the visitor to the hulks was grimly described by Howard. Apart from "their sickly looks", from which it was plain that "some mismanagement was among them", he saw that "many had no shirts, some no waistcoats, some no stockings, and some no shoes". On his second visit, fifteen months later, "there seemed to be no uniform plan with regard to their clothing; he perceived some had no shirts on, some looked as though they had not been washed for many weeks, some looked tight, some had shoes, and some had none, or such as they could not possibly work in". Where friends of the convicts were able to provide them with clothing, Campbell was quite willing to save his money; to the rest he gave a shirt of linen check, a brown jacket, and a pair of breeches—how long these garments were supposed to last was left unstated. The clothes in which a man first arrived from the assizes were, it was declared, "pulled off and thrown overboard"; but practice differed widely from theory, and it was truly a scarecrow collection of human refuse that was rowed ashore to work in the Arsenal.

At first the prisoners had slept in two tiers of hammocks, one above the other; next in a single tier—the hammocks, in either case, used to become entangled in their irons. As the hulks grew more crowded, platforms were erected along each side of the deck; by day, when not in use as tables, they would be placed upright against the walls, and lowered at night. Six men slept on each, with a mat beneath them and a rug covering each couple—little wonder that the hulks housed vermin of every sort. The space allotted to a sleeper was six feet in length and not more than twenty inches in width. As with clothing, Campbell was quite willing for friends to provide blankets if they wished. In the morning, when the men had been locked down, and moreover allowed candles, for ten hours in summer and twelve in winter, "he smelt no ill smell", he declared, and anyhow, there were river-side portholes which could be opened if desired. Some of his friends were not so positive about the lack of smell, but they made light of it on the ground that the vessels were usually well aired during the day.

Still, we are told—on the authority of Stewart Erskine, captain of the hulks—that the men were "contented with their beds", and in addition, "all seemed satisfied with the provision that is allowed them". Their diet consisted chiefly of ox-cheek either boiled or made into soup, pease, and bread or biscuit—on two days in the week, known as Burgoo Days, meat was replaced by oatmeal and cheese. The men were divided into messes of six, each mess being allowed half an ox-cheek (undressed) or two pounds of cheese, three pints of pease or oatmeal, and a quantity of bread or biscuit varying from time to time between four-and-a-half and six pounds. Each man had a quart of small beer on four days in the week, and water, drawn from the river and filtered (though imperfectly) on the others. Sometimes the ox-cheeks were "kept too long, and stinking"; they were served up just the same. After a year or two and a great deal of fuss, however, meat in that condition was usually returned to the sub-contractor and better substituted; which was just as well, since long before this friends had been stopped from supplying extra food, as it was found that they introduced saws and other instruments of escape into their gifts. To provide the vegetables which all the doctors declared necessary for health, Campbell bought a plot of ground near the Arsenal and employed some of his crippled prisoners as gardeners; this plot of ground continued in the possession of the hulks until about 1850, although more of its produce went to the officers than to the convicts.

But the article of diet which aroused the most acute discontent was the bread and biscuit. Howard told how, on his first visit, he waited to see the rations weighed out to some of the messes.

"The biscuit was brought in two sacks; one was all crumbs and the other broken. There were many whole ones and some pieces of three-quarters of a biscuit; they took out about two handfuls of crumbs, and the rest out of the other sack. He stayed whilst fifteen messes at least were weighed out; he saw all the biscuits were mouldy and green on both sides; the crumbs he could not see so distinctly, but he apprehends they were of the same sort."

When he visited the hulks again, however, he found the prisoners receiving "good wholesome bread". Dr. Solander, a botanist member of the Royal Society, "took some of it to the tavern, and he and the company with him preferred it to other bread". Sir Herbert Mackworth, a Member of Parliament, who had also paid a visit to Woolwich, "thought it very good for a poor man to eat". But though the quality had improved, the quantity had not; for men who were supposed to labour the rations were inadequate—they were still, moreover, "much tainted", although the convicts thought it wise to make their complaints to Howard "in a soft tone, so that nobody but himself could hear". It was, to say the least, impolitic to win from the officers the reputation of a malcontent; for officers could retaliate on all such hang-dog curs, and fifteen ounces of bread, half a pint of pease, and a sixth of an ox-cheek weighing about five-and-a-half pounds when undressed, was better than nothing and possibly a flick of the lash into the bargain.

Such was life in Campbell's Academy, as revealed to Sir Charles Bunbury's committee. But the most ominous phrase in the committee's Observations was that which recommended a continuance of the system, pointing out that "further beneficial alterations may be made in it, in case it shall be thought proper to be prolonged as a mode of punishment". No destination had yet been discovered for transported felons, and the temporary expedient of 1776 already looked like becoming permanent.

Chapter Three

ARISTOCRATS OF CRIME

YET only a few years were to elapse before the true nature of Campbell's Academy was realised. A Committee on Transportation in 1785 reported that "they [the hulks] form distinct societies for the more complete instruction of all new comers, who, after the expiration of their sentences, return into the mass of the community, not reformed in their principles but confirmed in every vicious habit". Some years later Patrick Colquhoun, an experienced London magistrate, declared that "as far as my observation has been directed to convicts who have been discharged from those establishments, I have seldom or never known of an instance of their return to honest industry; on the contrary, many of them have been detected immediately afterwards in the commission of new crimes, from which it may be inferred that this species of punishment has not answered the intentions of the legislature so far as relates to the reformation of the convicts; but the chief cause of the general corruption of morals, which is so apparent, has been traced to the indiscriminate mixture of hardened and irreclaimable thieves with country convicts who, under other circumstances, might have been reclaimed, but with so many evil examples before them too often become as hardened at the period of their discharge as the worst class of felons, thereby rendering the establishment a complete seminary of vice and wickedness".

All that Colquhoun said of country convicts applied with little less force to a handful of London ones—those who, before they were caught, lived well, slept soft, and called themselves gentlemen. In the gaols on shore, a man with money or influence could withdraw himself at least partially from the riff-raff; by bribery he often succeeded in obtaining quite unwarrantable alleviation of his lot. On board the hulks, with their single deck for all prisoners, no sort of bribery would be of use, no separation of prisoners was at that time attempted; by day and by night a man was forced into intimate association with the basest specimens of humanity.

Typical of this aristocracy of crime was a lodger on board the *Justitia*, Harry Sterne—"Gentleman Harry", as he was popularly styled. "He was very well dressed", according to the *Newgate Calendar*, "and being of an easy address, and tolerably educated, got admission to the best company, on whom he could advantageously levy his contributions." How Sterne reacted to the company he found awaiting him at Woolwich, we do not know; he died before his release. Some years later, Major Semple, or Semple-Lisle, adventurer and swindler, stabbed himself rather than face the ordeal. But the *preux chevalier* of the hulks during the closing years of the eighteenth century was George Barrington, who enjoyed such notoriety that he was twice mentioned by Sir Charles Bunbury's Committee—the only convict in whose fate the least interest was taken.

Born in Ireland about 1755, he came to London in early youth to study medicine. But his health was never good, and his industry deplorable; contriving to mix in high society, he turned pickpocket and in the course of only a few years brought off some astonishing thefts—notably when he stole from the waistcoat pocket of Count Gregory Orloff, the discarded favourite of Catherine the Great of Russia, a gold snuff-box set with brilliants and worth, it was said, between £30,000 and £40,000. During his prentice days, however, he had more than once come in contact with the law and been granted the benefit of a very dubious doubt; although the charge on which he was actually committed to Woolwich was an unsensational one, Barrington was sentenced to three years "on board the ballast lighters". He had the appearance, according to a descriptive reporter of the period, of being "a very genteel man, about 21, and very far from athletic: his hair dressed *a la mode*; clothes quite in the taste; a fine gold-headed taper cane, with suitable tassels, and elegant Artois buckles. In short he is the *genteelest* thief ever remembered to have been seen at the Old Bailey, and it is a *great pity* he should be condemned to so *vulgar* an employment as ballast-heaving."

To Woolwich he went, to the *Justitia*; and there, according to the *Scots Magazine*, "from an appearance the most genteel, [he] is become an object of commiseration. His behaviour is mild, humble, patient. He entertains a just sense of his dishonest course of life, and performs his lot with all possible industry in a state of true contrition." "His associate and friend, Miss West", we learn from the biographical sketch that precedes his own, or alleged, *Voyage to New South Wales*, was in his absence, "compelled to act and execute alone. . . . To soothe the gloomy hours of captivity as much as possible, she constantly sent to Barrington two guineas per week, and paid him personal visits as often as opportunity would permit. In one of these excursions she fell into the company of the celebrated David Brown Dignum, who then belonged to Mr. Campbell's Academy; and who, having plenty of cash, was selected as a proper object for the display of this lady's talents, and she actually perpetrated the deed in the midst of the seat of punishment, and congratulated herself not a little on the brilliancy of her success. But Barrington, who always strongly supported the common maxim, that there is honesty among thieves, compelled her to restore the plunder; though much against her inclination."

Since the name of David Brown Dignum has been mentioned (as it is also mentioned in the letters of Horace Walpole)* we may turn aside for the moment in order to deal with its owner. Dignum, "a very gentleman-like man and ill brooks the severity of his sentence", had been condemned to five years on board the hulks for receiving £1200 from a certain John Clarke, for "investing him with the office of Clerk of the Minutes in H. Majesty's Customs House at Dublin"—a position in which Mr. Clarke had not the smallest interest, except that it provided him with a salary for doing nothing. Dignum had also received £1000 from Josiah Brown "under pretence of causing him to be appointed writer in the *London Gazette*". In both these instances the dupes had been given impressive warrants purporting to be signed by the Home Secretary, Lord Weymouth, and counter-signed by his head clerk, Thomas Daw. Not content with frauds of this description, Dignum had caused Beaumarchais, the librettist of *Le Barbier de Seville* and *Le Mariage de Figaro*, to be falsely charged in London as a French spy, and had revealed to Lord Suffolk a wholly fictitious conspiracy against the life of the King, in which he embroiled several Members of Parliament who had refused to pay him blackmail.

After sentence had been pronounced, says the *Newgate Calendar*, "no time was lost in conveying Dignum on board the ballast lighter. Being possessed of plenty of money, and having high notions of gentility, he went to Woolwich

---

* 13 March 1777 to the Rev. William Mason.

in a post chaise, with his negro servant behind, expecting that his money would procure every indulgence in his favour, and that his servant would still be admitted to attend him. But this time he was egregiously mistaken: the keepers of the lighter would not permit the negro to come on board, and Dignum was immediately put to the duty of the wheelbarrow."

Says the contributor to the *Scots Magazine*: "Dignum has been ill for a week but it was given our correspondent to understand that he would be properly visited; and, if he was found to be feigning illness, a severe hand would be held over him, and his working time increased. It is true that when he first went on board, he hired a boat at a guinea a week, for his black servant to come backwards and forwards to him from shore; and, the first day he was there, he ordered a dinner to be brought to him from Woolwich. When it was brought, the overseer ordered his servant to take it back, and give it to the first poor man he met, for it should not come there. Mr. Dignum, therefore, as well as other defrauders, knows what they have to depend on if they once enter on board the floating academy."

In due course, though with no great haste, Dignum was examined and, since it was found that he was not "feigning illness", he was admitted to the hospital for such treatment as was considered suitable for felons. But, in addition to being inadequate, it was also too late, and within a short time he was dead from gaol fever.

And now to return to Barrington.

"In recompense for his exemplary conduct", and with two-thirds of his sentence still unserved, he was restored to liberty. The Committee on Transportation which sat in 1785, and whose report was quoted earlier in this chapter, commented on the fact that "when they [convicts from the hulks] regain their liberty, no parish will receive them and no person set them to work; being shunned by their former acquaintances, and baffled in every attempt to gain their bread, the danger of starving almost irresistibly leads them to a renewal of their former crimes". Barrington proved no exception; within a few months he was back on board the *Justitia*, condemned this time to five years.

His first imprisonment had made serious inroads upon a health never robust; and it also happened that the early part of his second visit to Woolwich coincided with the period of mutiny and upheaval which spread from 1778 into 1779. It may be that he attempted to escape; quite apart from that and from the retribution that would follow in its wake, there is no doubt that for the innocent as well as the guilty it was a time of stress, gloom and accentuated hardship. Barrington "either found his sufferings more intolerable or his situation to be more desperate than they appeared to him on his first confinement; a circumstance which is said to have determined him upon suicide: and in consequence of this impious resolution, he stabbed himself with a pen-knife. The wound, tho' deep and dangerous, did not prove fatal; and medical assistance being called in, and seasonably applied, a cure was effected. It was, however, effected very slowly; and the wound having been given in the breast, seemed in its effects, after nearly two years' continuance, to bring a consumption on the unhappy patient."

To any man in such a plight, conditions on board the hulks were terrible indeed. Barrington did not exaggerate when he said that "colds that I had repeatedly caught had ulcerated my lungs, and labour often exceeding my strength by day, and putrified air by night, had greatly reduced and wasted my frame. The surgeons finding that the usual medicaments were not sufficient, applied to the super-intendent, and obtained a milk and vegetable diet for me.

C

This was a regimen never allowed there, but like extreme unction to those that were at the point of death."

At the end of four years he was granted a pardon on condition that he immediately left the country and never returned to it. He went to his native Ireland; but the notoriety he had won in London had preceded him and he was compelled to flee. He crossed to Edinburgh, where the police were too sharp for his liking; thence to the north of England, slowly travelling south towards the capital, and doubtless hoping to find himself forgotten there. But scarcely had he reached it, in 1783, than he appeared once more at the Old Bailey, charged this time with "not fulfilling the conditions of His Majesty's pardon", and condemned to undergo the remainder of his former sentence. There was talk of sending him back to Woolwich; but his cry, "My Lord, my disease is of such a nature, it is not in the power of medicine to relieve me if I go down to that place, and certain death must be the result", struck a chord of pity in the judicial breast, and he was allowed to serve his eleven months' term at Newgate instead. On his release, he yet again resorted to his old ways—what else could he do?—and it was not until six years later, when he was transported to New South Wales, that he was able to benefit by that fresh start in life which transportation to the colonies, for all its shortcomings, did sometimes hold out to the felon. Emancipated in 1792 as the result of good conduct, he set purposefully to work there to retrieve some little from the wreckage of the past, and to employ his intelligence in ways calculated to assist rather than hamper social amenity and morality. In these efforts, and in spite of a predilection for the rum bottle, he won such success that when he died, in 1804, he held the responsible appointments of Superintendent of Convicts and High Constable.

Chapter Four

HARDENING INTO PERMANENCE

BY the end of the eighteenth century there had become apparent two reasons why the hulks should be abolished. They had been recognised, not only by idealists and reformers, but also by practical men, as in no measure reformatory; and a new colony to which to transport felons was being exploited.

Yet in vain might Howard cry that "the association of so many criminals is *utterly destructive* of morals". In vain might Patrick Colquhoun write of the hulks as "seminaries of profligacy and vice" which "vomit forth at stated times upon the public a certain number of convicts, who having *no asylum, no home, no character,* and *no means* of subsistence, seem to have only the alternative of joining their companions in iniquity and of adding strength to the criminal phalanx". In vain might even a Parliamentary Committee of Finance, which sat in 1798, report that "there is little hope that the individuals who have been exposed to the contagion of such immoral example, whether they shall be finally sent to New South Wales, or the periods of their sentences shall be suffered to expire here, will ever again become useful members of society, but on the contrary it is to be feared that when they shall be again discharged upon the public they will come more expert in fraud and more hardened in guilt". The very fact that transportation to Botany Bay and Port Jackson in New South Wales had been opened up in 1786 was made to strengthen the case in favour of the existing establishment. Among the evidence presented to the Committee of 1798 was a return showing that, of a total of 1864 persons awaiting the departure of another fleet to the new colony, 1449 were confined on board the hulks; and appended to this return was a note to the effect that "the reason why so large a number of convicts remain here under these sentences of transportation, is because it has been found inexpedient to send a greater number of convicts than have already been sent to New South Wales until that settlement shall have attained a greater degree of cultivation; and that transportation hither has always been gradual, and according to the advices received from that settlement of the capability of receiving them". There is practical wisdom in this; but the revealed total of convicts confined makes one thing plain. Far from likelihood of abolition, the number of hulks must have been increased.

At the same time, the "permanent" system advocated by Howard, Jeremy Bentham and others, by which convicts were to be housed in large and airy penitentiaries where they could labour in common but sleep each in a separate cell, seemed no nearer coming into existence. Acts were passed to authorise it, Committees formed to set it in motion, experts examined and cross-examined. In London a site was actually ready for purchase. But, when urged to agree to the price, the Treasury replied that "new measures were about to be taken in respect of felons, which made the hastening of the Penitentiary Houses less necessary"; an allusion to an Act by which imprisonment in the hulks was made a distinct punishment in itself, quite apart from transportation. Revised plans were prepared; but the

Treasury remained adamant. It was true that the hulks were far from showing a profit—the labour of the convicts was estimated to produce no more than two-fifths of the cost of their maintenance. But at any rate, they were cheaper than the erection of new prisons ashore and presented other advantages as well. England was by that time engaged in her long and exhausting struggle for existence with Napoleonic France. The cost of living rose steadily, and it must have appeared beyond question that there was neither money nor occasion for overhauling penal methods. At the very moment when their abuses were generally recognised they were left to take their place as a normal mode of punishment fundamentally because men were too occupied with other matters to worry about them, and too short of funds to enter upon the expense that their abolition would entail.

Sir Charles Bunbury's Committee had, of course, recommended changes—a shorter term of incarceration, separate vessels to house the sick, a special receiving ship, the appointment of chaplains, and the appointment of "an officer or magistrate" who shall "have authority to visit and inspect the hulks and make a report from time to time respecting the management and conduct of the Superintendent and the execution of the contract, to such court or person as may be appointed to receive it". Most of these recommendations were put, with greater or less enthusiasm, into operation—except the appointment of an Inspector: that was not to be for more than twenty years. Instead, the Superintendent—Campbell, in short—was required to keep certain records for annual production to the Court of King's Bench. This Court, it may be added, followed the example of the Middlesex Justices in ignoring both the records and the hulks; from all its minutes we learn precisely nothing of what took place at Woolwich and elsewhere. But when we turn to Howard, we find him as faithful and observant in his visits after the Bunbury Committee as he had been before it.

There is no doubt that the Committee gave Campbell a jolt. By the end of 1779, to be sure, both the *Justitia* and the *Censor* were no less overcrowded than formerly—the former now housed 256 prisoners, the latter 250, since two decks were used for their accommodation instead of one. But there was—what there had not been previously—a hospital ship, as well as another, aptly named the *Reception*, wherein convicts were lodged for five days and examined by the surgeons, before being drafted to permanent quarters.

"The prisoners on board the *Justitia*", wrote Howard, "looked healthy and well; the decks were clean. They had bedding; their provisions were good of the sort; and there were not any (as at my former visits) without shoes and stockings. I found the *Censor* below deck cleaner than the *Justitia*; yet, on carefully viewing the convicts, they had not so contented and healthy an aspect as those in the other; and a much greater proportion of this ship's company was sent to the hospital." He could, however, discover nothing to account for the greater proportion. At subsequent visits, in 1782, 1783, 1787 and 1788, the general condition of cleanliness seems to have been maintained; in addition, rations had been slightly increased and improved. Howard had consistently urged that "it would be highly proper that a table of their stated allowance should be hung up, and scales, weights and measures assigned to them, to check the pursers who give out their provisions". He had urged too that "there should also be a table of rules and orders, similar to that for prisoners of war, with a strict prohibition against profaneness, which, I am sorry to say, is particularly necessary for the guards of these convicts". His words bore fruit so far as ration tables were concerned; but he had then to complain that they were hung in a position from which no convict could see them.

As to the hospital ship, "the cleanliness and quietness of this hospital did honour to the conductor. It is to be wished that the patients had better nourishment, as that in many cases would be more salutary than medical prescription." But summing up, he declares: "I think it will be admitted that the mode of confinement and labour in the hulks is too severe for the far greater number of those who are confined in them. At the same time, there is no proportion of punishment to the several offences, and consequently no distinction of guilt; which many wise legislators have long lamented as an evil which wants to be remedied." And more sternly come the words: "I must repeat my complaint that such an assemblage is entirely destructive to the morals of young convicts: the profaneness of the prisoners is not properly checked; and some of the guards set them a bad example."

While improvements were being made at Woolwich, however, the evil had taken root elsewhere—at Portsmouth and Plymouth, under the contractorship of Duncan Campbell, both in the early 1780's.

Howard went several times to Portsmouth and Plymouth. At Plymouth was at first an old 70-gun ship, the *Chatham*, but it was soon replaced by the *Dunkirk*, which was "more commodious", and which housed about 350 convicts. On his first visit, in 1783, Howard notes that the prisoners appeared healthy and well, in spite of the fact that the bread allowance was less than it had ever been at Woolwich. He continues: "There are among them many fine young fellows, who all live in total idleness, although some useful employment might here easily be found." When he again saw them eight months later, their situation was not much better. "The prisoners were all in total idleness, except 6 or 7 who were making a boat for the captain. One ingenious man had made a small inkstand (which I have by me) out of a bone of his meat; but his knife had been taken from him. I saw some with Bibles in their hands; but there is no chaplain, nor any religious service. Here also some of the keepers, by their profaneness, set a bad example to the prisoners."

"Three miserable objects, for attempting to break out, were let down into a dreadful dark and deep hole in the bottom of the ship, where they lay, almost naked, upon a little straw; but having been thus confined for some weeks, upon their entreaties, I obtained their release."

In one respect, however, the *Dunkirk* materially contributed to the history of the hulks: she was the first vessel in which any sort of division of convicts into separate classes was attempted. Instead of the open decks usual elsewhere, she was divided into seven separate compartments, though upon what principle, if any, the convicts were classed, or by what means, if any, they were supervised, we do not know. Howard merely comments that "such a room at night, when the hatches were down, must be very offensive". Yet although probably he spoke no more than the truth, the experiment was of importance, even though its results were slow in making themselves felt.

Around Portsmouth (where the men worked with fair regularity) there was one hulk, an Indiaman called the *Lion*, at Gosport, and three—the *Fortunée* (a captured French frigate), the *Ceres* (at one time the receiving ship at Woolwich), and a hospital ship—at Langston Harbour. Of the *Lion*, Howard wrote that, "the ship was clean and the prisoners had a healthy and placid look; but they lay two on a bed, with one blanket. Here were several to be transported for life, and some whose sentences were for short

terms: amongst them were boys of only ten years of
As to the inmates of the *Fortunée* and the *Ceres*, "their
and beer were good, but they complained sadly of the meat,
and, indeed, not without cause; for the beef was very lean,
full of bones, and not half the allowance, viz., one pound
to each man before it was dressed".

"Both ships", he continued, "were clean, particularly
the *Ceres*. The *Fortunée* had a few sick in that part called the
hospital; but the *Ceres* had many more sick than the hospital
part could contain. Several had the gaol fever and a few
petechiae.* Six out of ten that went from Bedford were
dead, and two of the others very sickly and dispirited."

Here Howard breaks off to insert a terrible footnote:
"The gaoler at Reading told me, 12th July 1788, that of the
11 convicts whom he carried on board the hulks, 1st April
1787, all were dead but three. I have observed that convicts
from the country often pine away and die without any
apparent sign of illness; and that of equal numbers, from
the country and from Newgate, three or four of the former
die for one of the latter." Then, reverting to Langston
Harbour, he continues: "The convicts lie two on a straw
bed, with one blanket; and after one is taken ill his companion soon sickens. . . . There is not in general that
attention to cleanliness in the clothes, linen, and persons of
the prisoners on the hulks which is necessary to preserve
their health; for although some were decently clad in their
own clothes, others were in rags; many without shirts."

Applied to the hulks in general, "healthy" must, like
"cleanly", be regarded as a relative term, for all the improvements they had undergone. The magistrate, Colquhoun,
declares that, between 1776 and 1795, out of 5,792 convicts
serving their sentence on board, 1,946 had died—roughly

---

* A small red or purple spot in the skin caused by extravasion of blood, occurring
in certain forms.—Oxford English Dictionary.

one in three, as in pre-Bunbury days. And from the memoirs of a gentleman-thief named James Hardy Vaux, we derive a vivid picture of those improved conditions which must have contributed, by the depression they caused, to the piling up of so formidable a mortality. Vaux had been sent on board the old and worn-out *Retribution*, a captured Spanish 32-gun ship, at Woolwich, during the opening years of the nineteenth century, to await a second period of transportation to New South Wales.

"There were confined in this floating dungeon", he says, "nearly 600 men, most of them double-ironed; and the reader may conceive the horrible effects arising from the continual rattling of chains, the filth and vermin naturally produced by such a crowd of miserable inhabitants, the oaths and execrations constantly heard amongst them; and above all the shocking necessity of associating and communicating more or less with so depraved a set of beings. On arriving on board, we were all immediately stripped and washed in two large tubs of water, then, after putting on each a suit of coarse slop clothing, we were ironed and sent below; our own clothes being taken from us, and detained until we could sell or otherwise dispose of them, as no person is exempted from the obligation to wear ship-dress."

There is perhaps a suggestion of orderliness and method in this; yet we should not forget the notion current in Vaux's day of "reforming" the criminal by his imprisonment. He continues:

"I soon met many of my old Botany Bay acquaintances, who were all eager to offer me their friendship and services, that is, with a view to rob me of what little I had; for in this place there is no other motive or subject for ingenuity. All former friendships are dissolved, and a man here will rob his best benefactor, or even messmate, of an article worth one halfpenny.

[32]

"Every morning, at seven o'clock, all the convicts capable of work, or, in fact, all who are capable of getting into the boats, are taken ashore to the Warren, in which the royal arsenal and other public buildings are situated, and there employed at various kinds of labour, some of them very fatiguing; and while so employed, each gang of sixteen or twenty men is watched and directed by a fellow called a guard. These guards are commonly of the lowest class of human beings; wretches devoid of all feeling; ignorant in the extreme, brutal by nature, and rendered tyrannical and cruel by the consciousness of the power they possess; no others, but such as I have described, would hold the situation, their wages being not more than a day labourer would earn in London. They invariably carry a large and ponderous stick, with which, without the smallest provocation, they will fell an unfortunate convict to the ground, and frequently repeat their blows long after the poor sufferer is insensible. . . .

"As to the food, the stipulated ration is very scanty, but of even a part of that they [the convicts] are defrauded. Their provisions being supplied by contractors, and not by government, are of the worst kind, such as would not be considered eatable or wholesome elsewhere. The allowance of bread is said to be about 20 oz per day. Three days in the week they have about 4 oz of cheese for dinner, and the other four days a pound of beef. The breakfast is invariably boiled barley, of the commonest kind imaginable; and of this the pigs of the hulk come in for a third part, because it is so nauseous that nothing but downright hunger will enable a man to eat it. For supper, they have, on banyan days, burgoo, of as good a quality as the barley, and which is similarly disposed of; and on meat days, the water in which the beef was boiled is thickened with barley, and forms a mess called 'smiggins', of a more detestable nature

[33]

than either of the two former. . . . The beef consists generally of old bulls, or cows which have died of age or famine; the least trace of fat is considered a phenomenon, and it is far inferior on the whole to good horseflesh. I once saw the prisoners throw the whole day's supply overboard the moment it was hoisted out of the boat, and for this offence they were severely flogged. . . .

"If I were to attempt a full description of the miseries endured in these ships, I could fill a volume; but I shall sum up all by stating that besides robbery from each other, which is as common as cursing and swearing, I witnessed among the prisoners themselves, during the twelve-month I remained with them, one deliberate murder, for which the perpetrator was executed at Maidstone, and one suicide; and that unnatural crimes are openly committed."

The deliberate murder to which Vaux refers is described in some detail in the *Newgate Calendar*, and affords a further insight into life in the improved hulks. The name of the victim, a fellow prisoner of the murderer, is not given; the perpetrator was William Colman, a young man only twenty years of age.

"A brick had, a night or two before, been thrown at one of the officers of the convicts, and the prisoner suspected that the deceased had given information that he was the man who had committed the offence. Being incensed at the deceased, he repeatedly swore he would be revenged. They were, however, apparently reconciled, shook hands, and drank together; the deceased also helped the prisoner into bed, as he was incommoded by being loaded with very heavy irons. It appeared, however, that the prisoner still cherished his purpose of revenge, for, after remaining in bed some time, when he supposed all about him were asleep, he softly rose and went to the place where he knew a knife was kept, which he got. He then stole to the bed of the deceased, and stabbed him in the throat and breast in the most determined manner. The wounds he gave were instantly mortal. He was, however, observed to have got out of bed, and to go to the place where the knife was, by the two convicts who gave evidence against him."

Chapter Five

"LIBERAL PRINCIPLES"

BY the time Vaux spent his year of imprisonment on board the *Retribution* at Woolwich, a far-reaching change had already been made in the management of the hulks. Duncan Campbell had gone; the Government shouldering part, at any rate, of its responsibility, had at last appointed the Inspector recommended by Sir Charles Bunbury's Committee nearly a quarter of a century earlier. In 1802 it chose Aaron Graham, a young magistrate who had won the good opinion of the authorities at the time of the mutinies at Spithead and the Nore.

Newer and larger vessels were taken into service in place of the older and smaller ones (except the *Justitia* at Woolwich), and a separate hospital ship was attached to each hulk depôt. Plymouth abandoned its hulk; but at Sheerness the *Zealand* was established about 1810, and thenceforth the Medway became a permanent hulk station. Contractors now supplied no more than food and clothing for the various depôts, the Government finding ships, guards, and officers, and imposing its own discipline; but in trying to graft this new system upon the old, so many administrative loose ends were left exposed that any benefit from it was, at first, almost lost. Yet Graham did increase rations, so that men were fed better than they had ever been on board the hulks; did form a convenient chapel in each ship; did substitute hammocks, in which the men lay singly, for the former platforms holding any number up to half a dozen. He did, moreover, make an effort at classifying prisoners, not by dividing the various decks into compartments, as in the old *Dunkirk* at Plymouth, but by providing separate companion ways to each deck, so that communication between them was impossible. In her time, the *Dunkirk*, housing 350 convicts on two decks, had been the largest hulk in the service, while under Graham's administration three housed as many as 500; it will thus be seen that the attempt did not, after all, materially improve upon its predecessor so far as the number of men in each division was concerned. But whereas in the *Dunkirk* freedom to move from one to another was almost certainly allowed until bedtime (and probably exercised after bedtime), under Graham's plan the separation was complete and absolute from the moment the hatches were closed down early in the evening. But Vaux's *Retribution*, the largest vessel at that time in the service, had to be omitted from the scheme on account of her age and unsuitability.

Thus far only was the reign of Aaron Graham as Inspector of the Hulk Establishment productive of genuine good. In the Public Record Office is a letter, dated 1813, concerning contracts for food to be delivered to the hulks and written on behalf of one of the contractors. It is of little interest except for the statement that "it is to be observed that the contractors for supplying the Convict Establishment have conducted the concern on liberal principles, and have never failed to attend to any suggestion of the Inspector, with a view to remove all causes of dissatisfaction among the convicts".

"Liberal principles" seems to have been the phrase best describing, not only the contractor's estimate of his own efforts, but also that of Graham himself where the whole Establishment was concerned. In the Annual Report which he presented to the Home Secretary in November 1814 (the last he made) he declares with something like unction that "the Captains, Officers and Guards of the Hulks have behaved with their usual kindness and humanity. . . . The Chaplains report very favourably of the devout attention and behaviour of the convicts during the performance of the Divine Service and their moral conduct on all other occasions", while "the Surgeons report all the Hulks to be in a healthy state". The days had, we are asked to believe, long passed when the hulks were seminaries of profligacy and vice; under Graham they had become nurseries of reformation and virtue. He does, it must be admitted, show in his returns a boy eleven years old on board the *Laurel* at Portsmouth, two boys of twelve on board the *Retribution* and the *Portland* at Langston Harbour, one of thirteen, four of fourteen, four of fifteen, and nine of sixteen—a total of 112 boys of nineteen and under: yet so long as the hulks were conducted on their present "liberal principles", what harm could possibly come of that? Graham was not a bad man—child labour was practised by God-fearing industrialists long after his time. But since the hulks had ceased to be a temporary, and therefore novel, expedient, both legislators and public lost interest in them. Graham, in short, had things very much his own way. It took a Select Committee which sat in 1811 and 1812 to rouse him.

Its terms of reference were to inquire into the laws relating to penitentiary houses; and although it was therefore more directly concerned with land prisons, it devoted close enough attention to the hulks to reveal, once again, the rottenness of the system and the laxity with which it was being conducted.

The old-established evil of insufficiency, or bad organisation, of labour on shore, still persisted. At Sheerness, for instance, there was not "regular employment at present in that yard for more than about 200 out of about 500 which that hulk [the *Zealand*] generally contains; but there does not appear to be any precise rule by which the Captain determines which individuals shall go ashore, or settles who shall do the ship's duty. . . . The Captain says that he takes those for work on shore in the morning who come forward, and that they in general prefer to go to labour in the morning, that they may stay on board in the afternoon.

"The convicts in the ship, with the exception of a few shoemakers and tailors, employed in keeping the shoes and clothes of the others in repair, and of those engaged in the ship's duty, are allowed to be idle, or to work for themselves at their pleasure; the materials for their work are procured on their own account, and they dispose of the articles made either by sending them up to town or by selling them in the dockyard." At Woolwich, Portsmouth and elsewhere labour seems to have been in steadier demand; nevertheless, in all vessels private work was allowed to be carried on by permission of the Captain—a permission which the officers were not always slow to turn to their own advantage.

An equally serious haphazardness was exhibited in the allowances of various sorts made to the convicts during their sentences and at the time of their discharge. At Woolwich, for example, each man received beer and other extras to the total value of from 2d to 4½d a day according to the class in which he was rated. In the Portsmouth dockyard the articles allowed were estimated at 2¼d a man, or 2¾d to those who used tobacco. Prisoners employed at Gosport and Langston Harbour had a daily allowance of biscuit, tobacco, and beer, to the value of about 1d each man; at Sheerness, on the other hand, nothing at all was allowed.

D

Similarly, when prisoners left the hulks they were given, at Woolwich and Sheerness, half a guinea, together with a suit of clothes; at Portsmouth and Langston Harbour, they received £1 16s 4d, but no clothes; and if discharged on a pardon, only £1. To those who were employed as artificers in the Ordnance Department at Cumberland Fort, Gosport, a gratuity of from one to five guineas was given from the Department itself at the expiration of their sentences, provided that they had conducted themselves properly.

Chaplains had long ago been appointed to the various hulk depôts; but that they too seem to have been infected by the prevailing random methods is strongly suggested by this extract from the Committee's reports:

"With regard to the attendance of the Chaplain on the hulks upon week days, it is mentioned in the 20th Article of the Instructions to the Captains, that 'the Chaplain is to visit the sick in the hulks occasionally, and to show himself ready and desirous to administer to them such spiritual advice and consolation as they may stand in need of'; which duty appears to your Committee to be executed; and the Captain is directed 'to give him timely notice of the death of any convict, so as to ensure his attendance at the funeral'; but except this Article, which must be considered as an incidental mention of some of the most important duties of the Chaplain, rather than as an instruction containing a summary of their whole duty, there does not appear to exist any specification in writing of what is required from the gentlemen who fill these situations. . . . It appears, from the examination of the Chaplain of the *Retribution*, that he considers his duties as confined to those above described, and does not think it necessary to endeavour to have personal communication with the convicts, except in cases of sickness."

As to the Portsmouth depôt, "it appears to your

Committee, on considering the Chaplain's evidence and comparing it with the accounts given of these hulks by the Captains, that the communication of this gentleman with individual convicts can hardly extend beyond a comparatively small number, who may apply to him voluntarily for instruction, or may hope, on particular occasions, to procure his good offices in their favour; or who may be desirous of consulting him upon their private concerns; and that of even of the real character of these, he can, according to the plan upon which the hulks are now conducted, have no means of forming a satisfactory judgment".

But it is of the practical results of such spiritual ministration and of Aaron Graham's liberal principles that the Committee's report paints a truly gruesome picture.

"It appears that from the time at which the convicts are locked down within their several decks in the evening, until the hatches are opened in the morning (a period which in winter includes nearly two-thirds of the twenty-four hours) they are left entirely to themselves without any of the officers or guards of the ship to inspect them, and without any other control over their conduct than the knowledge that any riotous noise or disturbance will be communicated by the guards, who are on watch in other parts of the vessel, to the officers, and will be followed by their interference. One or two of the convicts themselves are selected by the Captain of the hulk to act on each deck as boatswain's mates, whose duty it is to take care of the lights kept burning on the deck, and to call out to the watch from time to time that 'all is well'; and if the guard has any observation to make upon what is going on below, he addresses himself to these persons, but they exercise no authority over the other convicts, nor would they venture to mention openly to the Captain any irregularity or offence of which their fellow prisoners should be guilty. The Captains state themselves to be in the habit of communicating privately with many of the convicts, from whom they obtain intelligence concerning the character and behaviour of the rest, but it seems admitted that the individuals from whom such information is derived cannot be brought forward to prove the facts, from the danger to which they would in that case be exposed of being ill treated by their companions. Neither the Captains nor any other officer ever visits the parts of the ship in which the prisoners are confined, after the hatches are closed down, except upon some extraordinary emergency, or in cases of disturbance, which very rarely occur. And it seems doubtful whether, in some of the hulks at least, an officer could go down among the prisoners at night without the risk of personal injury. The guards never go among them at night."

A pretty state of affairs indeed—from one half to two-thirds of the twenty-four hours, the tail appears to have wagged the dog. The report proceeds:

"Under these circumstances there can be no doubt of the prevalence among the convicts (while thus left without restraint upon their behaviour) of gambling, swearing, and every kind of vicious conversation. It is stated, as the opinion of some of the persons examined by your Committee, that they do not often ill-use each other; but the fear of personal injury, which is known to prevail in the minds of many of them, to such an extent as frequently to stifle complaint, even in the case of theft, leads to a contrary conclusion; the Captain of the *Captivity*, on being asked whether convicts often complain of having been ill treated at night by their companions, says, 'it is a thing they dare not do in the *Captivity*, but in the *Laurel* (which he formerly commanded) they used to bring them up manfully'. The Captain of the *Portland*, who states that instances of their maltreating each other after they are locked down are very rare, adds, on being asked whether a convict maltreated by his companions would venture to complain, 'if marks of violence appear they know it would be observed; sometimes they do not tell me; but I see the mark of violence, and I call on them, and then they tell me'. The same Captain states, upon the subject of the manner in which convicts employ themselves at night, that if any noise like rapping or hammering is heard after a certain hour, they are desired to go to bed, it being known that they are making money, hammering out crowns and half-crowns into sixpences, the manufacture of which he represents as having been carried on by the convicts for some years."

With such a prelude as the foregoing, the climax ought to have been powerful indeed—nothing less than the sending up of the hulks in fire and smoke, and the transference of their inmates to decently built and well conducted prisons. "Under the circumstances which have been stated, your Committee cannot but consider the situation of the convicts imprisoned on board the hulks, upon their present plan, as one from which these persons must be expected to return into society with more depraved habits and dispositions than those with which they went into confinement; although it may happen in these, as in all other places of punishment, that the sufferings of the offender may in some instances awaken reflection and lead to amendment."

Then our eye alights upon the ominous word, "however".

"Your Committee, however, are not prepared to recommend that this Establishment should be discontinued, but on the contrary, are of the opinion that, on a revision of the system, it will be found practicable to introduce into it such alterations and corrections as will in a great degree lessen, if not altogether remove, the evils that now exist. In some respects the hulks possess advantages over any other place of confinement. The expenses of fitting up a vessel for the reception of prisoners and of keeping it in repair bear no proportion to the cost of erecting a Penitentiary House or House of Correction on shore. And the circumstance of the hulks being removable from place to place affords a convenience which can be found in no other description of prison; and of which it is hardly possible to calculate the value, with reference to the employment of convicts, since it gives opportunities of employing them in hard labour in behalf of the public, wherever their services may from time to time be required, in the neighbourhood of any port or navigable river, in which situations there is commonly a demand for labour of that kind."

And more in the same strain.

The Committee of 1811, in short, chucked away everything to save the life of a shibboleth—the shibboleth of "advantageousness". It would be unfair to forget the stress of war, under which its members sat; yet as we read the report, the impression grows upon us that the Committee, like previous Committees, saw its duty but burked it—with an ounce more courage, an ounce more moral force, the hulk system might have been brought to an end. Inevitably after this, its recommendations fall flat—even such important ones as further classification intended to "place the prisoners under the constant inspection of an officer or guard", the putting-by of a small sum from the produce of the convict's labour to be given him on discharge, the offer of dockyard work as a free workman after the expiry of sentence, and the appointment of another (and presumably more vigorous) head to the Hulk Establishment. At the close of 1814 Aaron Graham retired, his place being taken by John Henry Capper, whose name is more closely associated with the hulks than any other; during thirty years he ruled over them.

Chapter Six

PRISONERS OF WAR

ONE other consideration may possibly have weighed with the Committee of 1811 in recommending the retention of the hulks—that it would be illogical to abolish them for civil prisoners when at least a score were at that very moment housing prisoners of war.

The Seven Years War (1756–1763) had seen the establishment of the *Royal Oak* at Plymouth, later moved to Portsmouth. The War of American Independence had seen their renewed use on a slightly larger scale. It was the enormous number of prisoners brought to this country between 1793 and 1814 that, in addition to filling every prison camp and liberating numbers on parole, called into service a total of more than sixty hulks. We may perhaps believe that, over all this period, government intentions were not inhumane—at any rate, diplomatic correspondence (especially with neutrals) shows, broadly speaking, an attitude of benevolence. But jobbery, bribery and double-dealing made hay of good will. Contractors and agents feathered their own nest at the expense of prisoners with surprising impunity. Slackness and corruption invaded the Transport Office, which had the care of prisoners of war in its hands. It thus became wilfully ridiculous for John Wilson Croker, Secretary to the Admiralty, to declare to the House of Commons in 1812 that the prisoners at Portsmouth were "comfortable and happy and well provided with amusement", or for Sir George Warrender to repeat much the same story about those at Chatham. The impression left upon the minds of all who had the misfortune to be confined in these same hulks was a terrible one.

Forgetful of the execration its predecessors had brought upon their heads, it may be interpolated, the Government of a later day established a prison ship, the *Cape St. Vincent*, at Lisbon after the Carlist rising in Spain during the 1830s. Conditions on board appear to have been bad, the commander tyrannous. In October 1837 the occupants sent a petition to Queen Victoria, praying for amendment and relief. This petition, though the Government would have suppressed it, touched the young Queen's heart, and Captain Drake, of H.M.S. *Donegal*, was sent under instructions from Rear-Admiral Sir John Ommaney to inspect and report upon the hulk. "I do not consider," he wrote, "that more restraint is used towards them than is usual under such circumstances." Nevertheless steps were hurriedly taken to effect their exchange—possibly the standards he had adopted too closely resembled those of the Napoleonic wars.

Many of the hulks then employed were large vessels. Some had been captured—the *Vryheid*, for instance, (which served at Chatham) had been Admiral de Wynter's flagship at the battle of Camperdown in 1797, and later on, a good many French and Spanish vessels falling into our hands at Trafalgar and other sea fights. Our own old men-of-war went to swell the numbers—among them the *Sandwich* (90), *Nassau* (64), and *Belliqueux* (64), which had been prominent in the mutiny at the Nore in 1797; it was on board the *Sandwich* that Richard Parker, the leader of the mutiny, had been arrested, court-martialled, and shot, and in another hulk, the *Eagle*, that many of the mutineers had been imprisoned before she was used for prisoners of war.

A sketch of the hulks on the Medway as they appeared (not altogether accurately) to a captive is given by Captain (afterwards Baron) Charles Dupin in a report submitted to the French Government after his restoration to liberty.

"The Medway", he wrote, "is covered with men of war, dismantled and lying in ordinary. Their fresh and brilliant painting contrasts with the hideous aspect of the old and smoky hulks, which seem the remains of vessels blackened by a recent fire. It is in these floating tombs that prisoners of war are buried alive—Danes, Swedes, Frenchmen, Americans, no matter. They are lodged on the lower deck, on the upper deck, and even on the orlop deck. . . . Four hundred malefactors are the maximum of a ship appropriated to convicts. From eight hundred to twelve hundred is the ordinary number of prisoners of war heaped together in a prison ship of the same rate".

At Chatham (as well as at Portsmouth), it should be added, the hulks—half a dozen at each place, moored stem to stern—lay off a foul marsh, which periodically overspread them with its miasma and engulfed many would-be escapers in its slime.

In succeeding chapters we shall describe more fully the experiences and impressions of other prisoners; for the moment let us turn to those from whom we might expect to see the hulks in their most favourable light—the travelling Commissioners sent by the Transport Office to inspect the various depôts and to report to the Admiralty upon them.

Take a report at random—that of Commissioner Rupert George, written at Rochester in 1807. Under the direction of Captain Hutchinson, "I found the *Sandwich*, in which there are 708 men, of whom 18 are in the Sick Berth, in the most perfect state of cleanliness, and the Provisions, viz., Bread, Beef, and Soup, very good of its kind; the Meat, the Lieutenant informed me, is much better than the Ship's Company is supplied with from the Victualling Office." So far so good; but he concludes: "The Violence of the Wind prevented me from visiting the other Prison Ships, which I have no doubt are in a State at least equal to the *Sandwich*, as she is the oldest Ship and has the greatest Number of Prisoners on Board". Surely an unwarrantable assumption on the part of a gentleman who had been sent to inspect them all? Commissioner Rupert George, having earned a knighthood, became in due course Chairman of the Transport Office, and a person of importance. And while he occupied that position we find repeated year after year complaints of slackness and negligence on the part of local agents appointed by the Transport Board to supervise the needs of prisoners.

In 1801 the agent at Portsmouth, T. M. Slade, lived for the greater part of the year in London and left all the work to his clerk; while in Plymouth, at about the same time, the state of affairs is described by Commissioners W. A. Otway and James Johnston: "We visited the *Bienfaisant*, *Europe*, and *Prudent* Prison Ships, on board the former are Dutch, and in the others French Prisoners, these last were in general much in want of Necessary cloathing and bedding, tho' it appeared the Commanders of the Ships had made repeated application to the Agent for their being supplied. . . . The Dutch prisoners are in want of only a few articles of clothing which they shall be supplied with directly. . . . The particulars of the unpardonable negligence of Mr. White, the Agent, in seldom visiting the Prison Ships, and the consequent inattention of the Stewards to their duty, we shall not trouble their Lordships with."

[48]

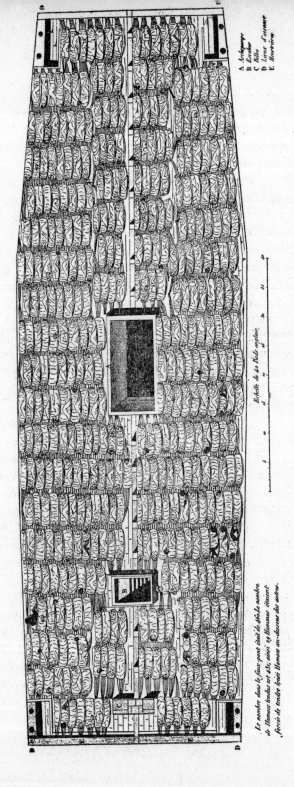

VUE DE L'INTÉRIEUR DU PONTON LE BRUNSWICK.

A. *Archipompe*
B. *Escalier*
C. *Bitte*
D. *Lieux d'aisance*
E. *Manœuvre*

Echelle de 50 Pieds anglais:

Le nombre dans le faux-pont était de 461, le nombre
de Hamacs tendus est 431, ainsi 29 Hommes étaient
forcés de tendre leurs Hamacs au-dessous des autres.

Hammock plan, Orlop deck of *Brunswick* prisoner-of-war hulk at Chatham, 1813

Some years previously, in 1796, Commissioner Otway had been concerned in the case of another agent, Mr. Dyne of Chatham. The prisoners on board the *Hero* and the *Bristol* had threatened mutiny if their grievances were not examined, and Otway was sent down to inquire into their principal allegation, that Dyne had systematically defrauded them of their rations. Dyne claimed that if at any time the prisoners had run short of provisions, the fault was not his but the contractor's, and that he did not possess sufficient authority to insist upon punctual delivery. He admitted that for nine months (the prisoners alleged sixteen) he had issued no soap, but said that it was in consequence of a theft of soap which had to be made up. He denied that he had received money from prisoners to procure them favourable positions in the lists which regulated their exchange with English prisoners in France; and on this point Otway thought it prudent to remain non-committal. Dyne was removed from his post.

There were, however, plenty of his kidney left. Woodriff, of Portsmouth, when he made an issue of clothing to the prisoners, used to buy it back from them at a cheap rate and then sell it again elsewhere. Yet he was at least conscientious to the point of making an issue at all; when asked whether it were not true that less than a quarter of the proper clothing had been served out at Chatham, Commander Mansell, head of the prison-ship police at that depôt, replied, "I am afraid it is true, but I have nothing to do with it. I cannot help it."

Seldom do we derive from the Commissioners' reports an impression of that overcrowding which was one of the worst features of the civil hulks; on the contrary, we find numbers of such statements as that "the prisoners are very healthy and the Ships upon the whole in tolerable good order". Occasionally mention is made of a lack of beds, and, after an inspection at Plymouth in 1801, "on board the hospital ships there are . . . in all 400 Patients, although the Ships are not calculated to contain with Propriety more than 300". According to the occupants, overcrowding was habitual, even deliberate. When Colonel Lebertre arrived as a prisoner on board the *Canada* at Chatham in 1811, he found no sleeping place vacant to receive him, and had to buy one for 120 francs from a fellow captive more anxious for money than for comparative comfort. Newcomers were often obliged to sleep on the bare deck and, when they did manage to acquire a hammock, only six feet were allowed in which to swing it. In the *Brunswick* at Chatham, supposed to be a good ship, the length of the orlop deck was 125 feet, the breadth 40 feet at the waist, and the height 4 feet 10 inches—into this space 460 prisoners were crowded at night; moreover, there was hammock space for only 431, so that 29 were compelled to sleep on the deck board. Fourteen portholes, each 17 inches square, barred but unglazed, admitted what air could enter this horrible den; even in winter it was hot and stinking, while in summer it became so unbearable that the inmates went about naked in order to obtain relief. So foul did the atmosphere grow by morning, after the prisoners had been locked down for ten or twelve hours, that, it is stated, a candle refused to burn, and the guards who removed the hatches were, as a matter of course, nearly overcome by the sudden outrush of reek from below.

This almost total absence of ventilation had for a long time been plain to the Commissioners, and we find many demands for windpipes and trunks to lighten the air in the lower decks—demands so often repeated, and repeated so urgently, that it seems obvious they produced no adequate response. At the same time, perhaps, it was an ill wind (or rather, lack of wind) which blew somebody some good;

in December 1796, Commissioners Otway and Johnston wrote from Portsmouth: "We have directed all the Blacks and People of Colour in health at Portsmouth to be removed into the *Captivity* and *Vigilant* Prison Ships, being the only ones now ready, the warmth and comfortable situation of the Spaces allotted for their accommodation between the different Decks we trust will prevent the effect the cold had hitherto on them at the prison." The previous winter had been very severe; the situation of the West Indian prisoners, mulattos and blacks, Commissioner Otway had written, "is truly melancholy, being rendered Cripples for Life by the loss of Toes, Fingers, etc., etc., some are even deprived of both Feet . . . many others I apprehend will meet a similar fate if detained in this Country, as it is absolutely impossible to guard People of that description from the effects of a climate so very different from their own".

Whether their transference from Porchester to the hulks proved as beneficial as the Commissioner had hoped is, however, to be doubted, for the mortality on board the hulks in general, though difficult to determine accurately, was undoubtedly high, and the percentage of those who were liberated broken in health was higher still. A London newspaper, reporting on a medical inquiry, is said to have declared that even the strongest men must be physically wrecked after six years on board; there were many who had exceeded that span and some who had doubled it.

One wonders what was the fate of the boys who had been unlucky enough to fall into English hands and be sent to the hulks. In the Public Record Office are several papers mentioning them; one, dated 1798, gives a list of youngsters in the *Royal Oak* at Portsmouth—three of 10 years of age, three of 11, and six of 12, most of them captured on board fishing boats or small privateers. In the *Prothée*, also at Portsmouth, were 105 boys—three of them were only 9 years old, five were 10, and thirty-two were 11. Some weeks later another batch was received, three of 9, one of 10, and six of 11. In 1801 there were 301 boys on board the *San Ysidro* at Plymouth. What happened to all these waifs of war whose early lives were blighted by the brutality and folly of their elders and betters? That they were, for the most part, hardy is true, for all that we meet such descriptions as "very small", and "small for his years"; that, in the company of men chafing under horrible conditions and galling idleness, their minds were corrupted is terribly certain, although somewhat half-hearted attempts were from time to time made to segregate them. That many died affords almost a feeling of relief—they, at any rate, were beyond the reach of harm and misery.

Commissioner H. Towse, writing from Chatham in 1806, comments: "The Prison decks washed alternate days, which I conceive too frequently". What with inadequate issues of clothes, prohibition of bathing, shortages of soap, skimped rations, and overcrowding, little wonder that the hulks were alive with vermin, that skin diseases and lung troubles were rampant, that depression and debility caused the occupants to sink to the lowest level of manhood. "Life on them", wrote a prisoner, "is the touchstone of a man's character." But on the other hand, "the general appearance of the Prisoners is uncommonly strong and healthy, and is satisfactory Proof of the present Ration to a Prisoner of War being, when fairly and regularly consumed by him, sufficient to preserve him in Health, provided he take proper care of himself". Thus declared three Commissioners —B. S. Rowley, A. Serle, and J. Harness—at Rochester in 1801. Easier it is for us to credit the word of Lieutenant Gardiner, newly appointed to command the *Europe* hulk at Plymouth, who wrote in 1796 to the Lords of the Admiralty:

"I beg to state for their Lordships' information the wretched situation of at least 300 of the Prisoners now on board of the *Europe* under my command, they are destitute of almost every Article of Clothing and all that many have is a miserable piece of dirty old Hammock sewed round their bodies, without Shoes, Stockings, Shirts, without so much as a covering to the head or a handkerchief to the *neck* and to compleat their misery they have not had an ounce of Soap issued to them these three weeks and *upwards*. The Surgeon of the *Europe* has represented to me that the Prisoners are becoming sickly and that he is apprehensive that some Serious Disorders may ensue if Clothing is not issued to them at this inclement Season of the Year [November]; and also hopes that their proportion of Soap might be continued to keep them clean.

"I trust their Lordships will believe me when I assure them that I have used every argument and endeavour in my power to obtain relief for these miserable Prisoners before I would presume to trouble their Lordships upon the subject, but sorry I am to add that all my endeavours have not only been in vain but very unsatisfactory. To the Eastward [Portsmouth and the Medway?] each Prisoner was served Four Ounces of Soap pr. week, here on the contrary they never receive more than two ounces and for these three Weeks and upwards they have not had any. Finding the Prisoners in this wretched state, I have made a very diligent and minute inquiry to find whether they had any Clothes issued to them from an Idea that they might have made an improper use of them but strange as it may appear to their Lordships I cannot find by the Prisoners nor the joint testimony of the Officers of the Ship that any Articles of Clothing has ever been issued to them."

Gardiner is to be remembered as among the more humane hulk commanders in the service; although it is not necessary

Discovery as a hulk at Deptford, 1828

to accept the word of those prisoners who asserted that every officer had been drawn from the dregs of the Navy, the fact does seem undeniable that all but the pick of them were tainted with the idea that any treatment was good enough for an enemy. They ranged from martinets to arrant rogues. Commissioner Otway wrote from Plymouth in 1799, "on inquiry into the Character and Conduct of the various persons employed at the Prison and on board the Prison Ships, they seem to be as fit for their respective Situations as under all the Circumstances can be expected"— hardly a recommendation of which any man could feel proud. Fourteen years later, in 1813, Commissioner A. Boyle, at Portsmouth, enters into greater detail: "Lieut. Harley of the *Suffolk*, I found extremely drunk at 10 o'clock, and I understand that is generally the case with him. Lieut. Peding, 2nd of the same ship, is also a most Drunken Character. Lieut. Voller, 2nd of the *Guildford*, who is absent on leave, I should recommend to the Board to be immediately discharged for reasons unnecessary to point out in a Public Letter, but which I will communicate on my return."

According to the Baron de Bonnefoux, an ex-prisoner whose Memoirs appeared in 1835, Milne, commander of the *Bahama*, used to hold disgraceful carouses on board, during one of which he accidentally set fire to the ship— whereupon he ordered that the prisoners should be shot rather than attempt to save themselves. The list could be extended. But it is pleasanter to mention another man worthy of being ranked with Gardiner—Captain Miller, commandant of the Portsmouth anchorage, who employed a French officer to collect complaints from his fellow captives with a view to remedying them, and on one occasion, when a number of fishing boats had been captured by an English frigate, was so incensed by what he regarded as a violation

E

of the laws of humanity that he bullied the Transport Office into authorising the release of their crews.

It is scarcely surprising in the circumstances that surgeons too were often slack or worse. "The surgeons have not duly performed the services required of them", wrote three Commissioners from Portsmouth in 1801. "They have resided, and attended their private Practice, on shore." It was, indeed, not uncommon that the care of prisoners should be left to their assistants, who were very far from being qualified men and sometimes not even medical students. Often, one would imagine, the prisoners preferred it so; when the surgeon himself took a hand patients were wont to come in for disgraceful treatment. Towards the end of 1811 the *Vengeance* at Portsmouth received a batch of Frenchmen who, after imprisonment by the Spaniards, had been sent to the hulks in a deplorable condition—"thin as skeletons, pale as corpses, scarcely covered, although the cold was intense, by their miserable rags". Of the thirty of them, only about ten had sufficient strength to crawl on board; the remainder were left helpless in the open boat which had brought them alongside. The surgeon of the *Vengeance* having refused to receive them, they were left untended in the boat while arrangements were made with the commander of the *Pegasus* hospital ship to take them in. At first he too refused; but later relented on condition that they should be washed before arrival. So, on the order of the surgeon of the *Vengeance*, they were plunged straightway into the sea, then hauled on to the deck of the *Pegasus*, most of them in a dying condition.

Yet without doubt the most terrible and demoralising feature of life on board the hulks appropriated to prisoners of war was an idleness far more complete than ever obtained in those for civil criminals. Apart from a roll-call, and a few fatigue duties which required only a handful of prisoners, there was absolutely nothing to do; from one year's end to another, each day was passed in blankly and hopelessly awaiting the next. No opportunity for healthy exercise either of mind or body was provided by the authorities. The most enterprising of the wretched captives occupied themselves in giving or receiving lessons in mathematics, languages, dancing, or sword-play at a sou an hour; handicrafts, carried on with makeshift tools and smuggled materials, flourished and all sorts of trinkets were sold under pettily-conceived regulations in the neighbouring towns and villages. But for the most part, men lounged despairingly, engaging in vicious conversation, gambling with the ferocity of tigers, practising forgery (at which many were adept), or meditating new and ingenious ways of escape. A rough code of honour, upheld by solemn trials, retained some sort of discipline on board; but codes of honour were powerless to check the vice desperately prevalent throughout the hulks. Says the Baron de Bonnefoux: "There existed neither fear, reserve, nor self-respect among that class which could not claim the benefits of education. Among them reigned openly the most perverse immorality, the most shameful outrages to modesty, the most revolting of actions, the most unblushing cynicism, and, in the midst of the general misery, one added misery greater than can be conceived."

That misery on board was general cannot, in view of the evidence quoted in this chapter, be gainsaid; what seems incredible therefore is that visitors to the hulks were frequent—visitors from the shore, who rowed out in small boats, clambered on to the quarter-deck, and from that point of vantage watched the crowd of half-starved and often half-naked men on the deck below, known as the Parc. What is even more incredible is that many of these visitors appear to have been women. Colonel Lebertre comments on their demeanour: "Even the women displayed an indifference absolutely horrifying. They would stay for hours together with their eyes fixed on the Parc, where the prisoners were, and without this spectacle of misery, which would so sensibly affect a Frenchwoman, starting a single tear. On the contrary, an insulting laugh was on their lips. The prisoners have known only one instance of a woman who fainted at sight of the Parc."

Occasionally, it appears, women even lived on board, although no special provision was made for them. What manner of woman they usually were there is, of course, no doubt. Yet all do not fit into that category. In the Public Record Office is a letter (dated 1813) from T. B. Thompson at the Navy Office to Commissioner Bowan, which runs as follows:

"The Bearer is the *wife* of a Captain Douditt a French prisoner of war at Chatham whom I took the liberty of writing to you about some time ago. She wishes to be allowed to live on board the Prison Ship with her husband. Pray do me the favor to see her, and hear her wishes with a favorable ear if you can."

A covering letter from Bowan to Alexander McLeay, Secretary of the Transport Board, includes this sentence, "If the Board have no objection I think the Lady may be indulged"; and a postscript, "Have the goodness to tell T. Thompson what is done for his French Lady".

Chapter Seven

LOUIS GARNERAY

WHILE it is lamentably certain that the hulks wrecked thousands of lives, it is also certain that prisoners could make the best, as well as the worst, of their conditions. There was a privateer captain, Louis Garneray, who employed his nine years in the hulks, not only to perfect his English, so that he was appointed interpreter on board, and to train himself to the point of later becoming an artist of national merit, but also to write in after life the fullest account we possess of the experiences and impressions of a Frenchman condemned to waste the best years of his young manhood as a prisoner of war.

His father had studied painting under David; his brother, a pupil of Isabey, worked for the Empress Josephine and gave lessons to Queen Hortense. Louis too had begun to study under his father, but at the age of thirteen ran away to sea, served on board a dozen different vessels, suffered several shipwrecks, won promotion, and at last, in 1806 (at twenty-three years old), was captured in the West Indies, shipped to Portsmouth, and put on board the *Prothée* in Porchester River.

Characteristic of all French prisoners was a love of gambling. In his book, *Mes Pontons*, Garneray introduces us to the lowest of them, known as les Rafalés—literally "those under the weather"—who became so enslaved by the gambling fever that they would wager everything, including rations and clothing. Having lost, they would live on whatever crumbs and refuse they could find about the ship—"a live rat was a gargantuan feast to them". They would go in all weathers virtually naked until they could beg, borrow, or steal some already worn-out garments —not to wear but to gamble with. Though forming the very dregs of the vessel, they were regarded with terror by the other prisoners and with a sort of grudging considera- tion by the authorities, since they included the strongest and most hard-bitten men on board, and had, moreover, a loosely-knit organisation, ruled by an elected "king", which enabled them to wield a far greater influence than their moral worth entitled them to. At night they used to lie huddled together, spoon-fashion for warmth, in the most noisome part of the orlop deck. So covered were they with lice that they sometimes went by the name of les Manteaux Impériaux, in allusion to the innumerable bees embroidered upon Napoleon's state robes. Astonishing as it may seem, there were actually prisoners with self-respect and education who were anxious to join the disreputable brotherhood; "but", says Garneray, "it is not enough to wish to enter. First one must be received. The man desirous of being admitted must begin by selling all he has, and with every copper of the money thus obtained regale all the members of the society with beer and bread. Then he will be recognised as a brother, and will be given a large stone to serve him as pillow."

The gambling in which the Rafalés indulged was indeed a gamble with despair itself. But it was not confined to them. It was to be observed wherever French prisoners of war were congregated.

"There is such a spirit of gambling", said *The Times* in

1807, "existing among the French prisoners lately arrived at Chatham from Norman Cross [an important depôt near Peterborough], that many of them have been almost entirely naked during the late severe weather, having lost their clothes, not even excepting their shirts and small clothes, to some of their fellow prisoners: many of them also are reduced to the chance of starving by the same means, having lost seven or eight days' provisions to their more fortunate companions, who never fail to exact their winnings. The effervescence of mind that this diabolical pursuit gives rise to is often exemplified in the conduct of these infatuated captives, rendering them remarkably turbulent and unruly. Saturday last, a quarrel arose between two of them in the course of play, when one of them, who had lost his clothes and food, received a stab in the back.

"Gambling among the French prisoners on the several prison-ships in the Medway has arrived at an alarming height. On board the *Buckingham*, where there are nearly 600 prisoners, are a billiard table, hazard tables, &c;* and the prisoners indulge themselves in play during the hours they are allowed for exercise."

But it was not gambling alone which made prisoners look like "a generation of dead men rising for a moment from their tombs, hollow-eyed, wan and earthy of complexion, bent-backed, shaggy bearded, and of a terrifying emaciation"; it was sheer lack of food, which, declared Garneray, did more than anything else to arouse a hatred of England in French hearts.

"Our week", he says, "was divided into full days and fast days; the former were five in number, the latter two. The ration for each prisoner comprised a pound and a quarter of brown bread and seven ounces of beef. We were

---

* All of them presumably home-made.

supposed to be given the wherewithal to make soup for ourselves at midday, although for the greater part of the time we had to go hungry. To make it we were served out with three ounces of barley and one ounce of onion for four men, or else three ounces of leek and some salt.

"On the two fast days our rations, in place of soup and meat, consisted, on Wednesdays, of a pound of smoked herring and a pound of potatoes; on Fridays, of a pound of dried cod and an equal weight of potatoes."

But the fish, he continues, was usually so bad that it could not be eaten; prisoners were in the habit of selling their herrings back to the contractor at a penny each. The contractor thereupon put them again into store and then again distributed them—to be bought once more for another penny. Or the contractor could use salt water in place of salt in the baking of bread, which was "not fit for a dog to eat". Clothing contractors, according to Garneray, would provide hundreds of suits of the same size; they would provide boots that fell to pieces at the first contact with wet, hammocks that refused to support the smallest weight, blankets so thin as to be almost transparent. Twelve hundred suits were ordered for delivery at Plymouth by October 1807 as stock for the winter; by March 1808, only three hundred had actually been received, although all had, of course, been paid for.

Garneray resumes:

"Our meagre ration which, at the first glance, would seem sufficient to nourish a man, actually represented only just enough to keep him from literally starving to death. And for these reasons: firstly, we never received the whole of it, since the contractors, knowing well enough that our complaints would not be listened to, never failed to withhold at least a small part; and secondly, we had further to deduct a proportion as follows:

"1. For prisoners who, either for having attempted to escape or for damage done, were put on two-thirds rations.

"2. To pay for a newspaper which we smuggled on board and for which, naturally, we were charged three times its real value.

"3. Lastly, for subsequent sale, in order to help the funds of those contemplating escape.

"These deductions were made indiscriminately, in equal parts among all the prisoners, for a rule long established and religiously kept laid it down that every man should receive the same quantity in the general distribution."

It is impossible in a short chapter to do justice to Garneray's account, which is a book full of vivid writing and acute observation of men and things. No more than a few incidents can be recounted here, as typical of the rest.

On board the *Prothée* Garneray met an old friend, a Breton privateer captain named Bertaud, and the pair determined to escape together. Boring a hole in the side of the hulk, just above the water line—a favourite device, as we shall see later—they made their arrangements with the utmost care; one dark July night, Bertaud slipped out through the hole while Garneray prepared to follow. But a small haversack which Bertaud carried on his back became entangled in an unnoticed nail in the ship's side. In trying unsuccessfully to free it, Bertaud attracted the attention of a sentry, who fired and wounded him. The shot brought the whole guard to the scene; thereupon followed a piece of barbarity which, since Garneray is by no means sensational in his writing, we may accept as accurate. As Bertaud hung suspended from the nail, neither completely free from the hole nor yet able to drop into the water, the guard set about clubbing him with the butts of their muskets, continuing until the haversack at last gave way and he fell insensible into the sea. He was picked up and unceremoniously taken to hospital, where for twenty-three days he lay at death's door; having been "returned to duty" (if only there had been duty to return to) he and Garneray were soon planning another attempt.

This time, however, it was in mid-winter and bitterly cold. The two succeeded in getting away from the hulk, swam to a mud-bank, which they crossed on a pair of ski-like appliances of their own devising, and in due course managed to clamber, half frozen, on board a vessel lying in the tideway, which, however, turned out to be a Dane whose captain threatened to give them up. Bertaud attacked, gagged and bound him, and sprang overboard; but Garneray, by this time too exhausted to continue, allowed himself to be taken back to the *Prothée*, where he was flung, still dripping wet and more dead than alive, into the Black Hole—a cell six feet square at the very bottom of the ship, without light or ventilation, swarming with rats, cockroaches and vermin. It was visited once in each twenty-four hours to enable the guard to bring the half-rations to which the occupant was entitled, to take away the latrine bucket, and to examine the locks; for the rest of the time the prisoner was left to himself. It is not surprising that after imprisonment in the Black Hole, sometimes lasting for weeks, men died or went mad.

Garneray, fortunately, was kept there only a short time; on his release, he was horrified to see the body of his friend, already an object of interest to crows and ravens, stretched upon the mud-banks near Porchester river. He entreated the authorities to have it removed. At first his appeals were received with scorn; at last a boat put off from the ship. The body was reached. The sailors attached a rope to the leg and brought it alongside the *Prothée*. There it was left, still in the water and horribly disfigured, until next morning, when it was towed to the *Pegasus* hospital ship for final disposal.

Soon after this Garneray was transferred to the *Crown*, under the command of a Lieutenant Ross—"a little man about four feet ten inches in height, enormously fat, as solid as a bear, and with a monstrous neck supporting the most hideous square head that can be imagined. Red hair, eyes of an indeterminate grey-blue, a thin hooked nose, a mouth which stretched from ear to ear and whose thin lips were incessantly agitated by a sort of tic or nervous movement, a complexion the colour of mahogany, and cheeks terribly scarred by smallpox, completed the appearance of the lieutenant."

Ross delighted in persecuting his prisoners. Once, for example, five men had escaped. Although it was the depth of winter and snow was falling steadily, he mustered the remainder on the open deck for roll-call. But the number could not be made right—for the reason (which, of course, he was unable to perceive) that a means had been devised by them of getting a certain number counted twice. And each time that number varied—but all the while the adventurous five were making good their escape, since Ross was too occupied and bewildered even to give the alarm. For three days he was kept busy and increasingly furious, with roll-call after roll-call. At last, knowing that he was being tricked but still unable to discover how, he called up the floating fire engines in the harbour and ordered them to turn their hoses, first upon the assembled prisoners, then upon the decks below, so that hammocks, clothes, food, and everything else was soaked in a deluge of icy water.

Nor did he stop there. He caused all the prisoners to be transferred for a few days to another ship. On their return to the *Crown* they found everything they had cherished destroyed by his orders—as for Garneray, "I discovered my tubes of colours crushed underfoot, my brushes and pencils broken, my canvases torn to ribbons; the books we possessed, reduced to mere shreds, covered the ground like a light fall of snow". The prisoners, beside themselves with rage at such treatment, were on the point of open mutiny, and were dissuaded only by a few of their more level-headed members from seizing the ship on their own account and butchering Ross and his crew.

Between commander and prisoners this cold war lost nothing of its bitterness. Ross bought a huge Newfoundland dog and chained it up on the quarter-deck as an extra guard to raise the alarm, should anything untoward occur during the night; within a very short time the prisoners had succeeded in poisoning it. Whenever he appeared, Ross was greeted with a tornado of whistles, yells, and cat-calls—which created a scandal throughout the depôt. And so on. It was partly by such tactics, partly on account of a forgery said to have been committed by one of the prisoners, that the state of affairs on board came at last to the ears of the authorities; after an official inquiry, Ross was removed from his post.

Before this, however, there had occurred an incident which Garneray recounts with great gusto. As hulk interpreter, he was called into Ross's cabin one day, to find drinking with the commander a certain nobleman (whom he does not name) who offered a purse of twenty pounds in a boxing match between his negro servant, Little White, and any French prisoner. At first the disparity between the lusty nigger, with his "Herculean torso", "arms larger than his thighs", and "chest occupying the space of two men one in front of the other", and the half-starved prisoners, did nothing but rouse the anger of those below, especially when they heard bets being made, not as to who should win, but on how long it would take Little White to kill his opponent. Garneray at last found a quiet-spoken, mild-mannered Breton, Robert Lange by name, to champion the French cause; and eight days later the fight took place.

All the beauty and fashion of Portsmouth were present on the quarter-deck of the *Crown*; the ragamuffin prisoners crowded round the ring which had been roped off in the Parc. Little White exhibited his muscles amid English cries of admiration and French murmurs of impotent fury; the demonstration over, Ross sent Garneray to order Lange into the ring.

After a short while Lange strolled up, pipe in mouth, hands in pockets; in reply to Milord, who acted as referee, he said he didn't know anything about boxing, had no seconds, but was quite ready to begin—whereupon he threw off his coat and assumed a pugnacious attitude. It was explained to him, amid a good deal of laughter, that first he must shake hands with his adversary "as a sign of friendship".

"Shake this hand of mine with respect", exclaimed Little White. "It has already crushed several Frenchmen."

These words, when translated to him by Garneray, seemed to have a miraculous effect upon Lange; his eyes dilated and he seized the negro's paw. "Their hands entwined, their gaze fixed, their inflamed faces close to each other, the two immovable combatants resembled a group in marble.

"Slowly it seemed to me that the face of Little White took on an expression of acute pain. I was not mistaken. Suddenly, letting a terrible cry escape him, the negro bit his lips in agony, half closed his eyes, threw back his head, hunched his shoulders with convulsive trembling, and seemed ready to faint. All this time the Breton remained impassive; not a muscle stirred; he was like a statue.

"What was happening was so unexpected, so extraordinary,

[67]

that we could make neither head nor tail of it. At last Robert Lange gave us the clue to the riddle.

" 'Wretch', he cried in a loud voice, addressing the negro, 'this hand which has killed several Frenchmen shall not henceforth frighten the smallest child.'

"And, indeed, with such apparently unbelievable strength had the hand of the Breton gripped that of his adversary that the negro's blood spurted from his fingers.

" 'Mercy, mercy!' cried Little White, unable to endure the agony any longer. 'Mercy! I am beaten. . . .'

"But Robert, heedless of the plea, deaf to such prayers, could not bring himself to relax his pressure, until the negro was on his knees before him. And then—hideous sight—we could see the hand hanging, inert and bloody, literally crushed by this terrible grip."

Towards the end of 1811, shortly before the *Crown* was taken out of commission, Garneray was transferred to the *Vengeance*, which, he tells us, was little better. The bugbear here was the surgeon, Dr. Weiss. One day, for instance, he dropped, as if by accident, a sheet of paper containing the names of forty captives about to be exchanged—whereat there was indescribable joy on board. Only later it was discovered that the paper was a hoax. Nor, according to Garneray, was Weiss's medical treatment of a much higher standard than his sense of humour; he consistently neglected his patients, approached them rather as a bully than as a doctor, and, had it not been for a colleague, Dr. Fuller (a very different stamp of man), would probably have lost the entire ship with fever. Once Fuller had effected the rescue, he was sent packing; little wonder that health on board the *Vengeance* was always low and that the hulk was ravaged by epidemic after epidemic. After only a short time on board, Garneray in his turn caught fever and was lucky to be sent to the *Pegasus* hospital ship.

While convalescent in the *Pegasus*, he saw enacted one night a gruesome incident. Two English hospital orderlies were closely watching a French soldier apparently at his last gasp. On one of his fingers, which were much swollen by disease, was a ring, probably his share of some pillage or adventure of war, and handsome enough to excite the greed of the orderlies. But the Frenchman would not, it seemed, hasten his dying and so give them the opportunity of stealing it at their leisure. With but little hesitation, they took the still living man to the mortuary, where he would pass for dead and thus enable them to chop off the finger. Fortunately Garneray was able to prevent the final horror; but he was told that such acts were quite normal on board the *Pegasus* and warned not to make a fuss about them.

In due course, he was admitted to parole at Bishops Waltham, in Hampshire, tried to escape, was brought back to the *Vengeance*, and was still in the Black Hole of that vessel when, one morning, the door opened and the turnkey entered.

" 'You can go out', he said to me very politely. 'You are free.'

"I got up stiffly and hurried on deck as fast as my weakness would allow. Judge of my surprise when, in passing by the battery, I saw my comrades behaving like madmen, dancing, embracing, weeping, and shouting inarticulately. For a moment I thought I must be in a dream. . . .

" 'What's the matter?' I asked an artillery sergeant, who, like myself, had been nearly ten years on board the hulks.

"To this question the sergeant offered no reply; but, falling on my neck, he pressed me to his heart, while his tears fell upon my face.

"Still more astounded, I repeated my question.

" 'Peace has been signed and we are free', he answered in a choked voice."

Chapter Eight

A YOUNG MAN OF MASSACHUSETTS

IN contrast to the despair into which the majority of French prisoners sank is the experience of those Americans who were taken after 1812, when the United States threw in her lot with France. They seem to have been regarded by their captors with a shade more sympathy than was displayed towards "those damn'd French monkeys", and (when not reviled as renegade Englishmen, rebels and traitors) with the sort of respect which took the form of "looking for more from you Yankees" than from the others. But they had also to thank their own aggressive nationalism, determination to stand up for their rights, and refusal to be put off with anything less—to say nothing, of course, of their much briefer period of captivity.

The fullest American version of life on board the hulks is contained in the "Journal of a Young Man of Massachusetts", which appeared in 1816. It was written by Dr. Benjamin Waterhouse, a New England surgeon, in the form of an autobiography; but there is no knowledge of its author's ever having been to sea, much less a prisoner, and the book may possibly be a compilation made from the first-hand tales of many returned captives. If this be so, it is superlatively good; as a picture, it carries conviction in every line, while practically all the facts that are capable of being checked are found to be accurate.

Waterhouse comments at some length on the differences between Americans and French. On board the *Crown Prince* at Chatham, where he declares he spent the greater part of two years, there were about 700 Americans and 100 Frenchmen.

"These Frenchmen", he says, "exhibited a considerable portion of ingenuity, industry, and patience in their little manufactories of bone, of straw, and of hair. They would work incessantly to get money, by selling those trifling wares; but many of them had a much more expeditious method of acquiring cash, and that was by gaming at the billiard tables and the wheels of fortune. Their skill and address at these apparent games of hazard were far superior to the Americans. They seemed calculated for gamesters. . . . Our people stood no chance with them, but were commonly stripped of every cent, whenever they set out seriously to play with them."

He admits, however, that they—in distinction to his own countrymen—kept sober, although, he adds, it was doubtless "in order to strip the boozy sailor of his money by gambling". Yet when more responsible Americans in the hulk tried to abolish the roulette boards, billiard tables, cards, and dice, which had led to so much misery and bad feeling, it was only after long exhortation on the one hand and surly threatening on the other that the reform was at last made. Educational classes were formed, the whole tone of the ship was raised. There had always been a Committee of twelve prisoners with an elected President to "make wholesome laws and define crimes and award punishments"; with no incitements to disorder, and with the Frenchmen subdued, the Committee found its authority increased and discipline stronger.

F

The commander of the *Crown Prince* was a certain
Lieutenant Osmore, who, according to Waterhouse, "had
been in the royal navy from his infancy, and now at the age
of 45 ranks no higher than a lieutenant. . . . He had an
amiable wife and many children, who lived in the prison
ship"—the amiable wife, it may be added, seems to have
been of a sympathetic disposition, often the chief bulwark
between her husband and mutiny. At one time rumour
circulated among the prisoners that Osmore had "taken
some sheep from the neighbouring marshes without leave
or licence, converted them to his own use, and that the
owner being about to prosecute him, the affair was made
up by the interposition of his friends, on compensation
being made". With the result that whenever he appeared
on his quarter-deck, or indeed anywhere about the ship,
he was greeted with cries of "Baa! baa!" from such prisoners
as were waiting for him. Incensed at what he considered an
insult, he ordered them to be driven below; but still the din
continued, being taken up now by the entire body of
captives and "sounding like an immense flock of sheep
that might have been heard a full mile". He therefore
forbade the market boats, which occasionally sold vegetables
and extra food of various sorts to the prisoners, to come
alongside, and for several days relations were so strained
that, in the end, two highly-placed port officials had to
negotiate, as it were, a truce between the parties.

That, however, was neither the first nor the last occasion
upon which there was trouble. One other instance must
suffice. Whenever a contractor omitted to send soft bread
on board, provided the weather did not forbid, he forfeited
half a pound a day to each man. Now the prisoners had
remained in ignorance of this regulation; having discovered
it, they determined to keep a sharper look-out in future.
On the first occasion that they made a complaint, Osmore

ordered an equivalent weight of hard bread—ship's biscuit
—to be served out instead; but the men refused to be put
off in that manner. Then "our commander swore from
the teeth outwards that if we refused his hard bread, we
should have none; we swore from the teeth, inwardly, that
we would adhere to our first declaration and maintain our
rights". Finding them obdurate and thinking them
insulting—Osmore was forever on the watch for insults—
he ordered them between decks; when, after a complete
day's hunger strike, they still persisted, he represented to
the authorities that they were in a state of mutiny, demanded
an extra guard, and sent his wife and children on shore.
But still the prisoners held out, "although to lay such an
embargo on our own bowels was, be sure, a pretty tough
piece of self-denial". At the end of a second day they were,
if the truth had been known, rapidly nearing the end of
their tether, when a couple of superior officers arrived on
board, instituted an inquiry, and discovering that "Mr. O.
had made representations not altogether correct", ordered
the hatches to be removed and the proper bread issued.
The prisoners had, in fact, won a victory, and Osmore
must swallow his wrath as best he could.

"Our situation in the day time", says Waterhouse, "was
not unpleasant for prisoners of war . . . the most un-
plesant during the night. It was the practice every night
at sun-set to count the prisoners as they went down below,
and then the hatchways were all barred down and locked
and the ladder of communication drawn up; and every
other precaution that fear inspires adopted to prevent our
escape, or our rising upon our prison keepers; for they
never had half the apprehension of the French as of the
Americans. . . . They had built round the side of the
ship, and a little above the surface of the water, a stage or
flooring, on which the sentries walked during the whole

night, singing out every half hour, 'all's well!' Besides these sentries marching round the ship, they had a floating guard in boats, rowing round all the ships during the live-long night. Whenever these boats rowed past a sentinel it was his duty to challenge them and theirs to answer; and this was done to ascertain whether they were French or American boats, come to *surprise* and carry by boarding the *Crown Prince*! We used to laugh among ourselves at this ridiculous precaution."

By morning, however, the atmosphere in the lower decks became almost unbreathable; which calls from Waterhouse the comment: "It is surprising, that after what the English philosophers have written concerning the properties of the atmospheric air; after what Boyle, Mahew, Hales, and Priestley have written on this subject: after what they have learned from the history of the Calcutta Black Hole; and after what Howard had taught them concerning prisons and hospitals—it is surprising that in the year 1813 commanders of ships in the English service should be allowed habitually to thrust a crowd of men into a space too small to contain half of them." But for all that, "we live pretty comfortably. . . . I believe we are nearly as well treated here in the river Medway as the British prisoners are at Salem or Boston"—although elsewhere he says, "not that we fare so well as British prisoners fare in America". Actually, of course, Americans and French were on an equal footing, so far as regulations were concerned. As to American morals, "such a sink of vice I never saw, or ever dreamed of, as I have seen here".

One of the things that most infuriated Waterhouse (next to the British in general and Scotsmen in particular) was the fact that many Americans on board the *Crown Prince* had not been fairly captured in battle but, previous to the declaration of war, had been impressed into the British

Navy from American merchantmen, without forgoing their American citizenship. When war broke out they, not unnaturally, had refused to fight and given themselves up as prisoners. A few commanders had appreciated such scruples, but, according to Waterhouse, the majority had resorted to measures of the utmost brutality in order to break down their resolution. Finding everything of no avail, they had at last sent them to the hulks. Such callousness, says Waterhouse, had embittered scores of lives past mending; and so had the discipline normally meted out to British sailors. "Several of those imprisoned men have declared that in looking back on their past sufferings on board English men of war, and comparing it with their present confinement at Chatham, they feel themselves in a Paradise." At any rate, a recruiting sergeant who appeared on board, offering prisoners sixteen guineas each to join the British army, met with no success—"we had a very good will to throw the slave overboard, but as we dare not, we contented ourselves with telling him what a flogging the Yankees would give him and his platoon when they got over to America". Nevertheless, some time later Waterhouse has to record "a disagreeable and mortifying occurrence".

"Four of our men agreed together to go on to the quarter-deck and offer themselves to the commander, to enter the service of the British. Their intention was discovered before they had an opportunity of putting it into execution. Two of them were caught, and two escaped. These two were arraigned and sentenced to be marked with the letter T, with India ink, pricked into their foreheads, being the initial of the word *Traitor*; after which, one went aft and entered; the other judged better, and remained with his countrymen. Had these been English we should have applauded them; had they been Irish, we had no right to blame them; but we had the mortification to know that they were by birth Americans."

A further cause of fury in Waterhouse and his fellow captives was the American agent at Chatham, Reuben G. Beasley. Beasley lived in London and there troubled himself not a whit about their welfare. Time and again they wrote to him, both individually and collectively, complaining of their conditions and begging the assistance it was no more than his obvious duty to render. He did not even answer their letters. Only once did he visit Chatham to see his charges. "He seemed fearful that they would come too near him", and "requested that additional sentries might be placed on the gangways to keep the prisoners from coming aft on the quarter-deck. He then sent for one of their number, said a few words to him relative to the prisoners; but not a word of information in answer to the questions repeatedly put to him; and of which we were all anxious to hear. He acted as if he was afraid that any questions should be put to him; so that without waiting to hear a single complaint, without any waiting to examine any thing respecting their situation, their health, or their wants, he hastily took his departure, amid the hoots and hisses of his countrymen, as he passed over the side of the ship."

During the winter of 1813–1814 smallpox broke out; whereat many of the prisoners refused to be vaccinated.

"I was surprised at this", writes Waterhouse, "until I found out that they felt no disposition to preserve their lives any longer. . . . Several of them told me that life was a burthen; that pride of character kept them from whining, and forced a smile on their countenance, while their being penned up like so many dirty hogs had chilled their souls, and sunk them, at times, into despondency. Some said that nothing but the hope of revenge kept them alive."

No sooner had smallpox begun to recede than there

came gaol fever—sure indication of the conditions under which they lived. "From four to six were taken down with it every day. We have about nine hundred men on board this ship; eight hundred of us wretched prisoners, and one hundred Englishmen. We are more crowded than is consistent with health or comfort. Our hammocks are slung one above another. It is warm and offensive in the middle of our habitation; those who have hammocks near the ports are unwilling to have them open at night. All this impedes the needful circulation of air."

Meanwhile the epidemic had spread throughout the depôt. "As the appropriate hospital ship is now crowded with sick, we are obliged to retain a number in the *Crown Prince*. The sick bay of this ship is now arranged like an hospital ship; and the hospital allowance is served out; and the chief surgeon visits us every week. Our Committee, composed of the oldest and most respectable men among us, do everything in their power to keep the ship and the prisoners clean." But still the epidemic spread; it was worst on board the *Bahama*. "One hundred and sixty Americans were put on board her in the month of January. She had been used as a prison for Danish sailors, many of whom were sick of typhus fever. These Americans came, like the rest of us, from Halifax; being weak, weary, fatigued and half-starved, their dejected spirits and debilitated bodies were aptly disposed to imbibe the contagion. Accordingly, soon after they went on board, they were attacked with it. All the Danes were sent out of her; and her upper deck is converted into an hospital; the surgeon has declared the ship to be infectious; and no one communicates with her but such as supply the ship and attend the sick." But these precautions came too late: "Out of three hundred and sixty-one Americans who came last on board, eighty-four were, in the course of three months, buried in the surrounding marshes, the burying place of the prison ships".

Then follows a bitter note:

"While *sick and imprisoned*, Mr. Beasley visited us *not*; but sent his clerk, a Mr. Williams, to supply the most needy with clothes. . . . This Mr. B. seems from the beginning to have considered his countrymen as a set of cheating, lying, swindling rascals; and a mutual contempt has existed between them. We wish our officers and agents would bear in mind this fact, that complacency begets complacency; and contempt begets contempt."

Gradually the gaol fever and accompanying epidemics abated; immediately there spread the rumour of a move—to Dartmoor, where the prison had recently been built, largely to relieve the overcrowded hulks at Plymouth. But the war had closed with the Allied entry into Paris, and the Hundred Days were not yet; prisoners of most other nationalities were beginning to be sent home, and the Americans had thus good grounds for discrediting the rumour. Nevertheless it proved to be true, and during the late summer of 1814 the first drafts began to leave Chatham for their prison ashore.

The draft, consisting of thirty men, had been due to leave the ship at night; their small possessions had been packed and their hammocks given back into store, when news came of a postponement. But instead of allowing them the use of their hammocks, Osmore replied that, since they were to start early next morning, they might sleep as best they could without them. Whereupon, directly he had gone to bed, the indignant prisoners began to drag forms, benches, any heavy but movable objects, from one end of their quarters to the other. They broke crockery against the bulkhead. They shouted, yelled, converted the ship into pandemonium. Osmore sent a marine to order them to keep quiet; they made more noise than ever. Osmore himself went, full of threats; these had no effect upon the rioters. "Then", said he, "I'll be damned if I don't fire on them." To which they yelled back, "Fire and be damned". Beside himself with fury, he returned once more to his cabin.

"Directly upon this", continues Waterhouse, "they collected all the tin and copper pans, pots, and kettles, and every sonorous metallic substance they could lay their hands on. These they tied together, and hitched bunches of them here and there upon the oaken planks; and then, with screaming, yelling like the Indian war-whoop, cheering, and the thundering noise of the planks grating along the deck, together with the ringing and clattering of the metallic vessels, they made altogether such a hideous 'rattle-cum-twang' that it was enough to raise all Chatham."

When the draft left next morning, they greeted Osmore with the usual cries of "Baa! baa!" keeping it up until they were out of hearing. As to Waterhouse, however, he was transferred first to the *Bahama*, now free from infection, which had on board about three hundred Americans of the lowest class—"I never saw a set of more ragged, dirty men in my life". There was no Committee here to keep them, or the authorities, up to the mark, and as the inevitable result, conditions were hideous. "Several persons now prisoners here", he says, "and I rank myself among that number, had a high idea of British humanity prior to our captivity; but we have been compelled to change our opinion of the people from whom we descended." Lieutenant Wilson, commander of the *Bahama* in succession to the egregious Milne, was a passionate, quick-tempered man, with, however, some remnants of a sense of justice. The mate was always drunk—and it was the mate who ruled the ship, when the commander of the neighbouring *Belliqueux* had not gratuitously taken over that duty.

The commander of the *Belliqueux*, having no one but phlegmatic and peaceable Norwegians to look after and finding time heavy on his hands, made a practice of spying on the *Bahama* from his own ship and reporting the slightest breach of regulations to Wilson. This was not long, of course, in coming to the knowledge of the prisoners; when next he appeared on his quarter-deck, he received several volleys of potatoes, the day's ration of the *Bahama*. In vain did he storm and threaten and come on board to insist upon punishment; Wilson took the matter with disconcerting coolness, and, as he stepped once more on to the deck of his own vessel, the commander of the *Belliqueux* felt another volley whistling through the air about him. While as for the prisoners, "we gained more by this short war than most nations of the world, for it entirely removed the cause for which we took up potatoes against one of his Britannick Majesty's officers, within ten leagues of the capital of his empire".

Chapter Nine

ALARUMS AND EXCURSIONS

G ARNERAY seems to have spoken no more than the
truth when he said that the question of rations, above
anything else, embittered the hearts of prisoners of
war. However good their food may have been according
to the regulations, it was often, in fact, deficient in quantity
and below contract standard in quality. Moreover, commanders were capricious in issuing or withholding it. The
evidence, where it is not to be found in our own official
records, is amply supplied in the notes and memoirs of
those who were expected to eat the stuff—as, for example,
in the *Carnets d'Étapes* of Sergeant-Major Beaudouin, who
was on board the *Sampson* at Gillingham from 1809 onwards.

"Half the time", he declares, "they give us provisions
which the very dogs refuse. Half the time the bread is not
baked, and is only good to bang against a wall. The meat
looks as though it had been dragged in the mud for miles.
Twice a week we get putrid salt fish, that is to say, herrings
on Wednesday and cod on Friday. We have several times
refused to eat it, and as a result got nothing in its place, and
at the same time are told that anything is good enough for a
Frenchman."

Repeatedly, as we have seen, prisoners protested to the
point of mutiny. Another instance occurred in 1808 on

board the *Bahama* under Lieutenant Milne. Several attempts at escape had exasperated Milne to such a degree that he ordered the entire ship to be put on half rations. This only made matters worse; scarcely a day passed without its disturbance. The climax was reached when bad weather prevented the delivery of bread on board, and biscuit was served out in its place. The prisoners assembled on deck, adopted a threatening attitude, and declared they would not disperse until proper rations had been served out to them. Milne replied with blood-curdling threats; when these were laughed at, he ordered them to be driven below at the bayonet's point. They refused to budge; whereupon he gave the command to open fire. Fortunately the officer in charge of the guard was a man of sense who refused to obey the order. On the prisoners' side, the Baron de Bonnefoux quieted them and then interviewed Milne on their behalf. Finding the opposition so united against him, Milne yielded, though with a very bad grace.

On the 31st May 1811 blood actually was spilt in the *Sampson* at Gillingham. The *Sampson* was set apart for re-captured escapers and those who had persistently given trouble in other hulks; discipline there was, naturally, stricter than elsewhere, but does not always seem to have been tempered by justice. During May the commander had had occasion to complain of damage done on board by some of the prisoners, and, not receiving satisfaction, had reduced rations. On the last day of the month matters came to a head. It is difficult to tell precisely what happened, for accounts are conflicting and no official report seems to exist; but the narrative of Sergeant-Major Beaudouin bears out fairly well the stories of others, some of whom were not, as he was, on board at the time, but in other hulks of the Chatham depôt.

"In the *Sampson*", he says, "the prisoners refused to eat

the food. The English allowed them to exist two days
without food. The prisoners resolved to force the English
to supply them with eatable provisions. Rather than die of
hunger, they all went on deck and requested the captain
either to give them food or to summon the commandant
of the anchorage. The brute replied that he would not
summon the commandant, and that they should have no
other provisions than those which had been served out to
them for the last two days. The prisoners refused to touch
them. The brigand then said: 'As you refuse to have this
food, I command you to return below immediately, or I
will fire upon you.' The prisoners could not believe that
he really meant what he said, and refused to go below.

"Hardly had they made this declaration than the captain
gave the word to the guard to fire, which was at once done,
the crowd being fired upon. The poor wretches, seeing that
they were being fired upon without any means of defence,
crowded hastily down, leaving behind only the killed and
wounded—fifteen killed and some twenty wounded. Then
the captain hoisted the mutiny signal, which brought
reinforcements from the other ships, and all were as jubilant
as if a great victory had been won."

Beaudouin appears to exaggerate the number of casualties
—it seems more probable that only six were killed, among
them an officer, though the estimate of the wounded varies
greatly. From another source—Dr. Fontana, French Officer
of Health with the army in Portugal, who was at the time a
prisoner on board the *Brunswick* at Chatham—we learn that
"the English did not forbear, after this massacre, in which
six Frenchmen were killed and six seriously wounded, from
maligning their victims; but their calumnies will one day
be refuted and the true facts brought to light. It will be
shown that they shot in the Parc poor half-starved wretches
who had been deprived of all food for twenty-four hours,

and who only demanded their rations, offering to pay forthwith the damage of which they had been accused, and even at the exhorbitant price at which it had been assessed by the English. These are certain facts; the report from which they are taken is signed by more than a hundred officers."

At the time, the affair was supposed to be connected with a plot to foment a simultaneous rising of all foreign prisoners in England—in the hulks, in the prisons and prison-camps, and on parole. But no evidence shows that it was, in fact, other than it seems—one sporadic outburst among others. No sense of guilt pursued prisoners of war, as it doubtless did civil criminals, when conditions were bad. The apparently interminable length of their captivity frayed and twitted the little nerve remaining to them, so that they were for ever on the edge of turmoil and crimes of violence. It is noteworthy, moreover, that the occupants of ships with the worst commanders seem to have been more effervescent than those of others. The *Sampson*, as we should expect, always bore a bad character. Another was the *San Damaso* at Portsmouth, while at one time the coroner at Rochester claimed treble fees from the Transport Office on account of the number of violent deaths occurring in the hulks at Chatham.

Among themselves, prisoners were always bickering and brawling. In 1812, for example, two captives in the *Sampson* settled a difference of opinion by descending into the Black Hole of the vessel and there fighting with razor blades lashed to sticks until one of them dropped dead. In the *Bahama* one man tried to snatch tobacco from another and was stabbed for his greed. During the early use of hulks for prisoners of war, a certain Jean Maneaux, on board the *Royal Oak* at Plymouth, was suspected of giving information to the authorities of an intended escape. His comrades tied him up and thrashed him with a rope's end to which a piece of iron had been attached. When he succeeded in bursting the cords which bound him, they jumped on him until his neck was broken, cut up the body into small pieces, and threw them overboard.

Garneray has the story of two members of the Rafalés whom he saw one day playing écarté surrounded by a silent and solemn crowd of onlookers. These, he was told, had been chosen by lot to murder the master of the hulk, Linch, a man universally detested for his overbearing manner; the play was to decide which of them should strike the blow. The game at an end, the winner rose and vanished; five minutes afterwards Linch lay dead on deck, with a knife through his heart.

On board the *Sampson* in 1813 three men were similarly chosen to do away with the master's mate and the sergeant of marines. The lot fell to Charles Manseraux; but having "compunction of conscience", in that the sergeant was a married man, he murdered a private instead, by stabbing him in the back.

Such incidents could be continued at length. They were the result of war passions suddenly deprived of an outlet; of hatred unable to dissipate itself in normal activity; but, more obviously still, of a nervous fury, combined with an intensity of despair, which counted death a happy, because speedy, end to indefinite confinement. At the same time, it was not always those who had been longest confined who were most ready to countenance violence; the very reputation of the hulks was sufficient for Baron le Jeune, who was taken to the *San Antonio* at Portsmouth in 1811. On his first arrival, "we ascended the side, and there, to our horror, we saw some five or six hundred prisoners, who were but one-third of those on board, climbing on to each others' shoulders, in the narrow space in which they were penned, to have a look at the newcomers, of whose arrival they seemed to have been told. Their silence, their attitude, and the looks of compassion they bestowed upon me as I greeted them in passing appeared to me omens of a terrible future for me". Le Jeune knew that in a few more steps he would be lost; he snatched a cutlass and threatened, to the loudly-expressed delight of the prisoners, to run through the body anyone who should attempt to detain him on board. This bellicose attitude alarmed the commander, who had its influence on his other captives to think about. The Baron was taken to the depôt at Forton instead, before being admitted to parole at Ashby-de-la-Zouche.

An alternative to violence, as a means of relief from the inaction and despair of captivity, was, of course, escape. In 1810 no fewer than thirty-two prisoners made off from the *Vigilant* at Portsmouth and only eight were re-captured. Other vessels had often to come alongside, and advantage could sometimes be taken of them. Thus in 1807 five men hid themselves in some empty watercasks that were being conveyed ashore for replenishing. In 1809 a French general tried to escape from the *Brunswick* at Chatham in a vegetable boat selling its produce to the prisoners. In 1812, also at Chatham, six Americans seized a ration boat alongside the *Canada*. During the war of American Independence two prisoners swam from the *San Rafael* at Plymouth to a lighter full of powder, overpowered the man in charge, and got away safely with her to France, where they sold the powder at a very handsome profit.

In the *Crown* the prisoners once held some theatricals, amongst the audience being a young British officer, newly arrived in the garrison, who lost his heart to the leading lady. In fact, he was rash enough to offer to see her home, and, when the offer was coyly accepted, gallantly led her down the companion-ladder of the hulk and made her comfortable in the stern-sheets of the gig. Only some time after they had reached the shore and were safely on the further side of Portsmouth did the ostensible lady reveal herself as one of the prisoners. The officer, faced with the prospect, if he gave "her" up, of making himself a laughing-stock throughout, not only the garrison and town, but the prisoners in the hulks as well, was compelled, however ungallantly, to connive at "her" escape.

The favourite method of escape was to cut a hole in the ship's side, just above the water-line and only large enough for a man to squeeze through on a dark night. Then followed an arduous swim to the shore, a perilous journey to one of the ports facing France, a scurried dash across the Channel in any boat which might happen to be left unguarded on the beach. All over the country there were escape agents, who would arrange the matter to the prisoner's satisfaction, though to a very considerable lightening of his pockets; there were countrymen and countrywomen who, with a human sympathy which put their betters to shame, would feed and hide escaped prisoners and send them on their way refreshed; and a good many smugglers carried on a more or less regular trade in assisting French prisoners to France and English prisoners back to England. All these, to be sure, laid themselves open to a long sentence in the civil hulks if they were caught; but they persisted nevertheless.

Typical among resourceful escapers was Tom Souville, of Calais, who was four times in English hands between 1795 and 1812 and three times successful in slipping through them, aided, no doubt, by an idiomatic knowledge of English. In these present days of thrilling escape stories from Germany and elsewhere his exploits may seem relatively simple; yet they demanded no less ingenuity, determination and coolness of head than those of the

G [87]

Second World War. The mudbanks off which the hulks lay at Portsmouth, where Souville was stationed, formed formidable natural barriers; equally formidable was the system by which news of escape was broadcast. It was usually, in the end, Souville's acquaintance with English smugglers that enabled him, having once got clear of the hulk and made his way from Portsmouth to Folkestone or Dover, to reach France.

Even there danger was not passed, if we are to believe his biographer. In 1808 he and a fellow captive named Havas succeeded in getting away to Calais. As they entered the harbour they saw a large and enthusiastic crowd awaiting them. At its forefront stood two impassive policemen; and as the heroes stepped on to the quay, the policemen approached with all the majesty of the law in their gait, and demanded passports. No passports being, of course, forthcoming, they were about to take Souville and Havas into custody, when the crowd, realising what went forward, pitched the policemen into the harbour and carried their countrymen shoulder-high to the Hôtel de Ville.

His last escape, in 1812, was made unaccompanied, again with a smuggler's help. With it his days as a prisoner in English hands ended; but after Waterloo he was placed in command of a cross-Channel packet and thus regularly visited these shores almost to the day of his death in 1840.

He survived by some twenty years the majority of the hulks that had scarred so deeply the minds of their captive occupants. One or two—notably the *Portland* and the *Captivity*, both at Portsmouth—had already been transferred in the early years of the century to the care of the Home Office for housing civil prisoners; the others were gradually drained of their miserable freight and broken up, though the notorious *Sampson*, empty but full of ugly memories, endured until the year of Souville's death.

Chapter Ten

THE REIGN OF J. H. CAPPER

WE must now return to the civil hulks, which, as we have seen, had not decreased in number, in spite of the drain upon the country, both in money and in men, made by the long and bitter war. By far the most interesting addition to the doleful fleet was the *Bellerophon*, the 74-gun man-of-war in which Napoleon was brought to England after Waterloo. On the 15th July 1815 he had surrendered to her commander, Sir Frederick Maitland, at Rochefort; on the 24th she arrived at Torbay, whence she was ordered to Plymouth to await the decision of the Government; and putting to sea again on the 4th August, Napoleon was removed to the *Northumberland* off Berry Head three days later, to be conveyed to St. Helena. As a hulk she lasted some nine years only and disappears from the records in 1825.

With the coming of peace, the Convict Establishment, excluding hospital and other attendant ships, comprised five vessels and 2429 convicts. This total was steadily to grow until, at the beginning of 1828, there were ten hulks and 4446 prisoners in England alone, in addition to others overseas. Thenceforward the numbers were to fluctuate according to the demands of the Australian colonies and the transportation policy of the home Government, but on the whole tended to diminish until 1840. Then the number increased again, until, three years later, a final ebb set in. By the middle of the century, and a few years before the hulks were abolished, the number of prisoners had dwindled to less than 2,000 and the number of vessels to four.

Another interesting addition was the *Discovery*, the vessel (of about 300 tons) that had accompanied Captain Cook on his last voyage. Under the command of Captain Clarke, she had left Plymouth in 1776, during the very month in which Campbell was first filling the *Justitia* and the *Censor* at Woolwich. Cook himself was on board the *Resolution*; the *Lion* and the *Dolphin* completed the little squadron. All had gone well until, while wintering in the Sandwich Islands three years later, Cook was murdered by a native. The *Resolution* and the *Discovery* reached the Nore in 1780; and for five years after 1791 the *Discovery* was employed under Commander George Vancouver (who, as one of Cook's midshipmen, had given his name to Vancouver Island) in exploring and surveying the western Canadian coast and the coasts of South America. About 1824 she appeared as a convict hulk at Deptford, and there remained for ten years, when her adventurous life was brought to a close in a shipbreaker's yard at Woolwich.

But if the hulks themselves were sometimes vessels which had been concerned in stirring events or great voyages, the officers and guards set to supervise their convict occupants consisted, speaking generally, of men of small calibre, though commonly of well-developed muscles and extensive vocabulary. To discover the detailed truth about them is not easy—even when they had the chance, convicts were chary of revealing much and the Superintendent had no wish to foul his own nest. Nevertheless it seems fairly certain that they were not always above receiving bribes either from prisoners or from prisoners' friends; they made small pretence at impartiality of treatment; they were often drunken, often careless, always ready to give a convincing demonstration of their power. Many of the officers seem, in their way, to have been little better, though of course more discreet in their methods; they cheated prisoners of rations and clothing, ordered the lash with a fine gesture of imperiousness, amended regulations to suit their own convenience, and sometimes maintained a discipline that was next to no discipline at all. One of them, however, went further. In May 1848 Richard Loader, overseer of the *Justitia* (the third *Justitia* to be used as a hulk), absconded with the sum of £750, the proceeds of two cheques which had been entrusted to him to cash at the Bank of England. It soon became known that he had been in the habit of borrowing money from his subordinate officers and that he had taken with him the watch and chain belonging to a convict, which, like the property of all prisoners, had been placed in his safekeeping during its owner's confinement. For several months there was a hue and cry after him; at the end of the summer he gave himself up to the police, stood his trial and was sentenced to seven years' transportation.

In short, it seems fairly probable that few of those employed by the Convict Establishment were the best men to place in command of prisoners whom the Government had expressed a desire to reform. Perhaps, to a certain degree, much the same might also be said of Home Secretaries.

They make a noble list—Peel, Melbourne, Sidmouth, John Russell, Lansdowne, Normanby, Sir John Graham, among others. Transportation (which promised Imperial and financial expansion), and development of prisons ashore, claimed a good deal of government time and thought; but neither Governments nor Home Secretaries felt called upon to bother themselves about the hulks, which thus assumed a good many of the attributes of a backwater. For many years after the Napoleonic wars, moreover, England was in a state of discontent and sometimes upheaval, which taxed the wits of all Ministers of the Crown. Under the superintendence of John Henry Capper, who, it will be recalled, had been appointed in succession to Aaron Graham as the result of the Committee of 1811, the hulks gave no trouble, and many a harassed Home Secretary might count himself lucky in possessing so faithful a servant.

For Capper, whose superintendence of the Convict Establishment lasted from 1814 to 1847, was a faithful servant indeed, although it is to be confessed that he appears strangely unbusiness-like in confirming on paper the orders and instructions he gave to his subordinates. It was less trouble to give them verbally, and throughout the thirty-three years he was in charge of the hulks correspondence concerning his work generally is of the meagrest —reminding us to a certain extent of the conspiracy of silence initiated by the Justices of Middlesex and maintained by the Court of King's Bench.

He did, of course, carry out reforms. It fell to him, for instance, at the very outset of his term of office, to put into effect the recommendations of the Committee of 1811, especially those which concerned the division of vessels into compartments intended to "place the prisoners under the constant supervision of an officer or guard". This cellular system was completed soon after 1815, and Capper, in his six-monthly report to the Home Secretary, declares that "the separating the prisoners of indifferent character, from those who are orderly disposed, has produced so great

a change that I have been assured by all the officers that
their duty in governing the convicts has been made comparatively easy to what it was formerly".

In most of the hulks a passage now ran down the middle
of each deck; on both sides of it were cells, containing from
ten to sixteen prisoners, opening on to the passage by a
door with a grille, through which all that went on within
could be seen. In the bulkhead separating one cell from
another was a lantern protected by a metal framework.
Every evening after supper the prisoners were locked in
their cells, and from that time until morning guards were
on duty in the passage to supervise them. How effective
this supervision was we shall learn in later chapters; at the
moment, it is the bare fact of supervision at all hours that
appeals to us.

When he was thus engaged in the *Retribution* (a second
vessel of that name), Capper found himself faced by a
difficulty, which he overcame in a manner all his own—it
appears, in a sense, symbolic of his whole period of office.
"I did not fail", he says, "to give due consideration to the
state of ventilation on board this ship; I found it necessary,
in order to admit a free circulation of air, to place at one
end of each of the two upper decks an iron-bar door opening
into the chapel, and also one in the orlop deck communicating with the steerage, which have added materially to the
ventilation." Nowhere, it will be remarked, does he really
increase ventilation to an appreciable degree; nowhere does
he admit any fresh air whatever, and the door communicating with the steerage must, at times, have allowed a very
strange substitute for it to enter the prisoners' quarters.
Still, the doors "have also afforded additional means of
overlooking the prisoners", and one suspects that this
advantage more than compensated in his mind for any
atmospheric deficiencies he may have noticed later.

Mention of cellular division on board the *Retribution* serves to introduce us to the Chaplain of that hulk, the Rev. Thomas Price. The following extract from a report written by him in 1816 shows him as a man of ideas:

"It was the frightful picture which I have been accustomed to view in the general depravity of the prisoners that led me about five years ago to submit to the consideration of the Penitentiary Committee of the House of Commons [the Committee of 1811] a plan for forming the decks of the ships into different compartments. . . . Although it was not adopted in the manner I proposed, yet I am thankful that any plan of division has been put into execution. Before this alteration took place, men were little known in the indiscriminate mixture; but now they are separated, classed and brought immediately into view. Before, when any robbery or crime was committed, it was in vain to look for the offender; he was either concealed or lost in a crowd; but now, if any dishonest acts are committed, or any vicious habits practised, they may be instantly detected."

Now one suspects that, of all men whom Capper would instinctively dislike, a man of ideas would cause him the greatest repugnance and anxiety. For Capper was not in the habit of suggesting things; he would carry out all that he had been told to do but, having no imagination, he had no real intelligence and, being forty years of age at the time of his appointment, was too old to develop either. Nor, apart from some years as clerk to Aaron Graham, does he appear to have had any special qualification for the post of Superintendent, a position which brought him in £400 a year. When first appointed, he lived at Lambeth Terrace (in the Lambeth Road, but now demolished) and carried on his work at home, an allowance of £131 a year being made for the use of his private residence as an office. Later, however, he gave up his house for this purpose and acquired

[94]

a room at the Home Office—but omitted to stop the allowance, which continued until his retirement. He used to employ convicts to do private work for him, and then forget to pay them. At first he was compelled to act as his own clerk; but in 1823 he obtained permission to employ one, and enlisted the services of his nephew, Robert Capper, at a salary (paid by the Government) of £270 a year. While acting in this capacity, Robert also carried on a grocery business in the Strand. As the years passed and his uncle's health began to fail, Robert took over virtually the entire superintendence of the Establishment; he visited the hulks in place of the old man, and his signature was recognised by officers and contractors as carrying the authority of the Superintendent proper. Just as John Henry was a faithful servant to Home Secretaries, so was Robert to John; and it could not have occurred to John to relinquish £400 a year, plus an allowance of £131, merely because ill health prevented him from himself performing the duties he had contracted with the Government to perform.

And perhaps, in so far as he was able to continue soothing occasional ministerial qualms of conscience, he really was worth retaining on the active list, for he had a useful knack of presenting the reassuring side of the Convict Establishment. It may be argued, of course, that in so doing he was safe-guarding his own position—that, for example, when in his six-monthly reports he declares the conduct of officers and prisoners to have been exemplary (as he not infrequently does), he intends the credit to be bestowed quite as much on himself as on them. A successful escape is passed over with the scantiest reference; but an unsuccessful one, though he obviously intends it as a black mark against the convicts in general, is more fully described—perhaps as showing the efficiency of the system. In discussing prisoners' health, he persisted throughout thirty years in maintaining that, whatever calamities might befall them on board, the real damage had been done before they came there, that it was the just consequence of their former vicious and profligate ways of life—thereby seeming to imply that little or no actual responsibility rested upon the hygiene of the hulks. The provisions are nearly always described as "good and wholesome", or by some similar phrase; and when, in 1817, the bread "has not been so good", he is careful to add that the cause "must be obvious to everyone"* and that the prisoners have no reasonable ground for complaint. In 1820, when the *York* was established at Gosport, she was stated to "have every advantage that a ship can possibly possess for the confinement of prisoners". And so on. It is, in fact, undeniable that, in being loyal to the serenity of mind of his Minister, he was also being loyal to his own interests; so much the better for him. When at last he left the Service he was seventy-two years old, and even his periodic reports were written for him by Robert. Robert was manifestly an apt pupil, but no doubt the old man was still careful to revise the final drafts.

The degree of his conscientiousness, however, is to be determined by realising the condition of the hulks during his reign. For the first few years he seems to have taken his duties seriously—every month he used to visit one or other of the depôts and spend at least twenty-four hours in examining everything for himself, beside being ready to listen to such complaints, from convicts as well as from officers, as were put before him. In those early days *The Times* once described him as discharging the "responsible and active duties of his office with a zeal, intelligence, and

---

* The Spring of 1816 was extraordinarily severe, and the harvest of that year was in consequence lamentably deficient. In his History of Prices (Vol. II p. 14) Tooke says that "nearly all the corn that had been saved was in so damp a condition as to be unfit for immediate use". Prices rose during 1817 to 103s. a quarter.

humanity which could not easily be surpassed". Gradually
the new broom ceased from sweeping so clean. His visits
were discontinued; such as were legally required were paid
now by Robert, but it became more usual for officers from
the various hulks to report to Capper at the Home Office.
For years he was almost entirely out of touch with those
whose welfare had been placed in his hands; and they
looked upon him with unconcealed contempt. It required
a tremendous upheaval to restore briskness and efficiency
to the Convict Establishment, grown torpid under his
influence; and the same upheaval that blew him sky-high,
and Robert with him, undermined the system itself, so that
in a few years it fell.

Chapter Eleven

ADVANCE—OF A SORT

ONE of the most beneficial reforms first noticeable during the 1820s is in the organisation of labour. We cease from hearing of men kept idle on board because there was nothing for them to do on shore. Portsmouth, the Medway, and the Thames employed their convict labourers steadily at dockyards and arsenals, and as work decreased in one place, so they, or a proportion of them, were transferred to another. Sometimes, when the rate of transportation slackened and waiting transports accumulated at home, a new depôt would be established— thus in 1825 the *Captivity* (a second hulk of that name) was brought from Portsmouth to Devonport, where an average of between 350 and 400 men were set to labour in the dockyard. Nine years later, when large numbers were once more being despatched to New South Wales, she, together with two other hulks (the *Hardy* at Tipnor and the *Retribution* at Sheerness), was abolished.

Actual transportation, it may be mentioned, was now contingent, not only upon the demands of the colony, but also upon the health and character of the prisoner. Unruly, physically strong, and long-sentence men were sent abroad at the first opportunity; others might, at the discretion of officers or surgeons, be allowed to serve their sentence in the hulks—frequently, it appears, a doubtful privilege, since it was declared in 1835 that "ninety-nine out of a hundred are very desirous of going" because "they say that their characters are lost in this country, and that there would be no possibility of their getting work if they go home". It therefore came about that the hulks often housed an abnormal proportion of old men and weaklings—thus far Capper's assertion, that the diseases prevalent on board were not due to conditions, may have had something to support it. For those who remained, sentences were divided into three periods, each decreasing in severity; but they all included labour ashore, at such tasks as loading and unloading vessels (including colliers and dredgers), constructing or repairing public works, excavating, stacking or carrying timber, painting ships, cleaning cables, and scraping shot—quite enough, one imagines, to tax the strength of a man who had been considered unfit to endure the rigours of a voyage to Australia in a convict ship. At any rate, ruptures and similar accidents were frequent at all depôts.

It is interesting to find in Capper's reports during the early 1820's references to the resentment of free labourers in the dockyards against the competition of convicts. The working classes were still struggling against low wages and a high cost of living, against an insecurity aggravated by the rapid introduction of machinery, and against laws which denied them the right to combine in their own protection. We can well understand their dismay at finding the available work reduced by convicts, whose complete absence of wages (except for a trifling allowance made by the dockyard) might well seem to threaten their existence. And indeed their fear may to some extent have been justified, for there is no doubt that the Government found convict labour financially attractive—even if it never paid the expenses of the hulks, it certainly reduced the expenses of the dockyards. But some tact appears to have been used in dealing with this problem; both at Chatham and at Deptford, where resentment was most openly voiced, the division between the two parties was carefully defined and maintained. At one time it became the rule to appoint free labourers as foremen of convict gangs, although afterwards this rule was changed back to one of rigorous separation.

But if objection was raised to convicts as competitors, no disapproval seems to have been made of them as fellow men; there was, indeed, constant fraternisation, much to the disquiet of Capper and the hulk officers, since its practical benefits were all on one side. Workmen were the usual medium for smuggling letters to and from the hulks; they placed spirits in the hands of the convicts, leaving it to the convicts to convey the liquor on board. Sometimes they aided in escapes; very late in the history of the hulks, both convicts and workmen at Woolwich used the same latrines in the dockyard, and more than one attempt was frustrated in which civilian suits were introduced and donned there, even in spite of the nearness of a warder. Many attempts were made to check collusion, both by increasing the number of guards and by aggravating the penalties of detection; but it continued nevertheless.

While on the subject of free labourers, it may be recalled that some of the early organisers of Trade Unions were sent to the hulks, notably the brothers Loveless, of Tolpuddle in Dorset, and their companions, who were sentenced to seven years' transportation for establishing a "Friendly Society" after their wages as agricultural labourers had been reduced to six shillings a week. Before the voyage to Hobart, they spent more than a month in the depôt at Portsmouth, most of them on board the *York*, where George Loveless "was struck with astonishment at the sight of the place, the clinking of the chains, and of so many men being stripped". The Overseer, however, seems to have treated him with a tact and sympathy which mitigated many of the hardships he would have had to suffer otherwise.

Another sign of increased orderliness and standardisation in the Convict Establishment was the fact that regulations and time-tables had become more or less identical throughout the various depôts. The following summary of a week-day in the 1830s on board the *Leviathan* at Portsmouth may be accepted as typical of the day on board all other hulks.

3.00 a.m.   Cooks rise to prepare prisoners' breakfast.

5.30 a.m.   All hands called.

5.45 a.m.   Muster on deck; breakfast; "then one of the three decks is washed, which is done every morning alternately".

6.45 a.m.   Each prisoner brings his hammock, stows it away on deck, and proceeds to labour. "On leaving the hulk their irons are examined by the guards, who also search their persons to prevent anything improper being concealed; and in order that they may be more strict in the execution of this duty, in the event of anything being afterwards found upon a prisoner, the guard that searched him is made responsible. . . . The prisoners are divided into sections of ten, each of which is subdivided as occasions, to make them more efficient, may require, and delivered into the charge of dockyard labourers. . . . The prisoners are overlooked by the First and Second Mate, who patrol the yard not only to prevent them from straying, or attempting to escape, but to make all parties attend strictly to their duties."

> At a quarter of an hour before the return of the prisoners on shore from labour, those employed on board are mustered to ascertain whether the number is correct.

12.00 noon   Prisoners return for dinner, and are searched to prevent any public stores being brought out of the dockyard; after which a general muster takes place. Dinners are served by officers, and the prisoners are locked up in their wards to eat it. A watch, consisting of an officer and half the ship's company, is set on and between decks, where they remain until 12.40, when the other half relieves them. (On board the *York* at Gosport, and later at Woolwich, convicts dined in sheds on shore).

1.20 p.m.   Prisoners return on shore for labour.

5.45 p.m.   On board again. Irons are examined, and their persons searched as in the forenoon. (5.30 in the *York*).

6.30 p.m.   School commences. (6.0 in the *York*; we shall have something to say about these schools in a later chapter).

7.30 p.m.   Prayers in the chapel; then all prisoners mustered and locked in their wards for the night.

9.00 p.m.   Lights out.

On Saturday evenings every prisoner was compelled to wash and shave himself in preparation for Sunday. Netx day, "all hands are called and mustered at the same time as on working days, the hammocks are brought up and stowed, and the decks cleanly swept, after which the prisoners return to their wards and breakfast is served. At 9 all prisoners are mustered in divisions on the Main Deck for the purpose of seeing that their persons and linen are clean, and their clothes kept in proper repair. The steward also during the week, as opportunities offer, sees that the repairing of the clothing is not neglected, and also issues clothing to those who need it."

Divine Service was performed once on Sundays by the Chaplain, who occasionally resided on board but much more often on shore. It was usual for the surgeon to reside on shore, and not infrequently to have a private practice, but his assistant always lived on board the hulk.

The irons worn by prisoners were now much lighter than formerly, although their weight could be increased as a punishment. Other normal—as distinct from severe—punishments included stoppage of the allowance made by the dockyard and a prohibition from receiving friends (a privilege officially accorded about once in three months, on a Sunday afternoon). Though prisoners were practically never discharged on medical grounds, a system of pardons to long-sentence men as a reward for exemplary conduct remained for many years in operation and, on the whole, probably had a beneficial effect on behaviour. It is true that we hear of this system chiefly through the hulk Chaplains; but though a Chaplain's word was not always to be taken literally, we cannot, of course, go so far as to disregard it. The Rev. T. Price, of the *Retribution*, for instance, reports that "I have received letters from several of those who have obtained their liberty by recommendations to the Royal Mercy; and it will be pleasing and satisfactory for you to learn, as it is gratifying for me to state, that they are settled and doing well". But we should be far more pleased and satisfied if we could learn the exact number of his vague 'several' for he seems flatly to contradict the testimony of officers from every depôt, when they comment repeatedly on the number of liberated men who return to the hulks like dogs to their vomit. In 1825 the *Times* declared that it was "a lamentable fact, that notwithstanding the severe lessons taught by the discipline of the hulks, very many instances occur of convicts who have been discharged again returning to the habits of dishonesty and again incurring the penalty of transportation".

About 1835 a system of reports from magistrates and land gaols to Overseers of the hulks, and from Overseers to the Governors of the Australian colony where the convicts under observation were sent, ensured, for actual transports, a continuity of treatment hitherto unattempted, and gave further inducement to good behaviour. When first arriving on board the hulks a man would be placed to sleep on the lower deck; as he progressed in the good opinion of the officers he would be promoted, first to the middle, then to the upper deck, which was much more airy and less crowded than those below. In the words of Peter Bossy, surgeon at Woolwich, in a report written in 1841, "the upper deck is much drier, being further removed from the surface of the river; and being more fully exposed to the sun, is hotter than the rest. The large size of its ports also affords better ventilation." Thus, by good behaviour a man improved his chances not only of comfort but also of retaining his health unimpaired, for the upper deck furnished a smaller proportion of sick than the others; the lower was dank and noisome, and the middle seemed to collect most of the permanent invalids and weaklings.

Yet, in spite of classification, standardisation, elaboration, and other efforts at bringing the system up to date—so that, as the *Times* once comically declared, "nowhere does good behaviour meet its reward more than at the hulks"—discipline on board remained inefficient and, though we do not hear much about them, disturbances were, at times, almost the order of the day. Thus in the 1820s a prisoner attempted to murder the Overseer of the *Bellerophon* and attacks on officers were of frequent occurrence; a quarter of a century later there were years of constant uproar, when the convicts in the *York* at Gosport went to the length of murdering a guard in order to obtain tobacco. Before 1832 the men were allowed to buy a small quantity of tobacco, which the surgeons "considered beneficial in fumigating the ship". After that date it was forbidden, and this deprivation appears to have been more keenly felt than any other. It was constantly smuggled from the shore through the good offices of free labourers, and a certain amount of trading in it went on between guards and prisoners, while a sort of rage engendered by lack of it habitually swelled the crime-list of every hulk. Once an officer ventured to urge the authorising of a small weekly allowance as a reward for good conduct, but his plea was not listened to.

Tobacco figured in a disturbance on board the *Warrior* at Woolwich on Christmas Eve 1846. Orders were given (it is not known by whom) that the men should be searched with greater thoroughness than usual when they went ashore to work, that their handkerchiefs (together, of course, with anything wrapped in them) should be taken away, and that cupboards and other receptacles in the various wards should also be minutely examined for forbidden articles. In this way a quantity of tobacco, coffee, and sugar was seized. When the men returned and discovered what had happened in their absence, they were, according to a guard who was present, "in a sort of mutinous state towards all the officers". They had, fortunately, been locked up before they realised the thoroughness of the search; they spent the evening in shouting, throwing all available missiles through the bars of the cells at officers and guards on duty, and threatening to break out and murder the Overseer and the First Mate. At last the Overseer, Henry

Masterman, went down among them and not only promised to give back next morning everything that had been taken, but also held out the prospect of a barrel of porter to be distributed with their Christmas dinner. Whereupon, of course, they subsided. At an inquiry held not long afterwards, Masterman told a highly surprising story to account for the porter which, like tobacco, was never allowed. But his story matters little; was not his reputation as an efficient officer already blasted when, under threat of trouble, he promised to return the goods that had been seized?

Even more serious was an attempt, made in 1829, to scuttle the *Dolphin* at Chatham. "Before any alarm was given", says the *Annual Register* (summarising the report of the *Times*), "the lower deck was covered with two feet of water, and at that moment two hundred human beings, buried in profound sleep, were locked in, totally unconscious of their perilous situation. There were nearly two hundred more convicts on the second deck, and in all, the vessel contained nearly five hundred persons." This estimate certainly does not exaggerate; the *Dolphin* was a large ship, and for many years had housed between 650 and 700 prisoners. The *Annual Register* continues:

"It was precisely one o'clock on Friday morning (16th October) when the *Dolphin* fell upon her beam ends. . . . In a few minutes the alarm was given that the vessel was sinking; a gun was fired as a signal of distress, the bells of the dockyard and garrison were rung, and blue lights were hung out on the mast of every vessel in the river. The troops of the garrison—in all, about two hundred—were mustered in about twenty minutes on the beach in the dockyard; and during that period Captain George Lloyd (of the *Dolphin*), the Quarter Master, and the boatswain were actively engaged in using all their efforts to save the lives of the convicts.

"About one hundred and fifty convicts had by that time escaped from the lower deck, many having been pulled through the portholes (the stanchions of which had been beaten in) and others having escaped up the gangway. Holes were also cut in the top of the deck, and also in the sides of the vessel; and through one aperture thirty-five men were taken out, almost dead. They had kept their heads above water for nearly an hour by holding to the tops of their hammocks. Before two o'clock nearly three hundred and eighty convicts, many of them perfectly naked, and none having more clothing than a shirt, were taken from the vessel and were marched along the beach by the military to a place about a quarter of a mile distant from the ship and contiguous to the hospital ship *Canada*."

It was presumably one or more of the convicts who had been responsible for the scuttling, though no report appears to exist of an inquiry into the affair. But throughout the graphic narrative of the *Annual Register* our mind returns to one question: what had happened to the keys that locked the prisoners in their cells? That they were not, apparently, available when most urgently needed may well be evidence of grave mismanagement.

Yet, if disorders of one kind and another were many, successful escapes seem to have been rare, although attempts were frequent. In giving evidence before a Select Committee in 1835, Capper told how, a short time previously, "there were four men rowed away from the Yard [at Woolwich], and one was found two days afterwards smoking his pipe among his old friends in Whitechapel; another had been heard of in Nottinghamshire; but the escapes are really astonishingly few, considering the number of men and the mode in which they are disposed about the Yard". Another witness said that "there have been numerous attempts within the last few years, but there have been only thirteen lost in four years and a half. Some have been brought back to the hulks, others taken for other offences."

Unfortunately we hear almost nothing about those numerous attempts. Apart from a few newspaper paragraphs which tell us little, we are compelled to fall back upon Capper's reports—and he does no more than mention an occasional "attempt made by a gang of convicts employed at the Royal Arsenal at Woolwich to effect their escape by swimming across the Ordnance canal", or "a desperate attempt by a few notorious London offenders prior to their sailing for the Australian Settlements, in which great violence was used". At Woolwich, the would-be escaper's aim (that is, if he had not merely changed his clothes and walked boldly out of the main gate with a crowd of free labourers) was generally to reach the Essex marshes, near to which there were woods in which he might feel himself, if not safe, at least able to give his pursuers a fair field. At Portsmouth he would scamper inland and hide in farm buildings, or make his way along the London road. It was impossible, owing to imperfect classification, which allowed men to concoct schemes without difficulty, to prevent these adventures on the part both of individuals and of small groups; but, in later days at least, the police of the entire neighbourhood were so quickly warned that success was almost out of the question from the outset.

Chapter Twelve

COCKS ON THEIR OWN DUNGHILL

SHORTLY before 1840 there came to the *Warrior* at Woolwich a well-educated convict from Staffordshire named Botham.

Now it was customary for the Overseer to appoint one of the convicts to act as his clerk. This was an entirely unofficial appointment; the clerk did no work on shore, and therefore received no dockyard pay but, on the other hand, probably earned small gratifications and ameliorations of various kinds which made up for the loss. The clerkship on board the *Warrior* had been held by a man named Blacker, to whom Botham, immediately on his arrival, became assistant, since Blacker was almost due for discharge. Before long, according to one of the guards, Botham "had the run of the ship, so that he was more a commanding officer than any other man I have seen on board yet". The prisoners were fully aware of his power; "the ship", the guard went on, "was continually in an uproar when this man was here; it was a continual uproar with the other prisoners, from the manner that he used to serve them. They used to say he was more like an Overseer than anything else."

He did not sleep in a ward or cell with the other men, but in the sick bay, where better beds were provided. He did not keep the same hours as they did; he appears, indeed, to have kept very much what hours he chose. Nor did he restrict himself to the usual convict rations; forbidden articles of food, which had been seized by the officers, seem to have found their way on to his plate. He was allowed to draw dockyard pay against all precedent. He used to sell certain positions on board to those prisoners who could make it worth his while—he was declared to have made one man a cook for ten shillings, and another a wardsman for thirty shillings paid in instalments; from those who could not afford to give so much he would be content to receive less, so long as he benefited somehow. From the poorest he would take bread—"a loaf or two for shifting a man" from one class to another. When they were sick, he would continue to credit them with dockyard pay and put it into his own pocket.

His power in the ship seems to have been due to an extraordinary influence over Masterman, the Overseer. If a guard offended Botham he offended Masterman—so, at least, averred one of the guards in the course of an Inquiry, held in 1847, which we shall discuss at length in its proper place. "It was felt generally by the officers", said another witness, "that he was in a situation quite incompatible with that of a prisoner, that he had more influence than some of the officers." Masterman, of course, was hot in his denials; having appointed Botham his clerk, he contended, he could not but repose trust in him. Beyond that, "he had no greater confidence in Botham than in other prisoners". If, however, any hint of undue influence was made by an officer on board, he (Masterman) "treated you in a manner that no officer ought to be treated".

No specific reason for this influence emerged from the evidence at the Inquiry. Yet the fact of it was both patent and objectionable, and most officers of the *Warrior*—

notably Henry Holmes, First Mate—were steadily on the watch for an opportunity of making a definite accusation against Botham, and so bringing matters to a head. The chance came at last. Holmes, in accusing Botham of selling to prisoners bread that was theirs by right, pressed Masterman to make a thorough investigation. Masterman did, after some hesitation, make investigation of a kind; but Botham's accounts, it was discovered, had been destroyed, and Holmes's papers, which would have substantiated his charges against the clerk, were stolen from the chest in his cabin while he was in the dockyard. In these circumstances Masterman brought in a verdict of Not Guilty, since, as he pointed out, the only remaining evidence came from convicts and was "therefore unreliable"; and for that reason too, he did not enter either the charge or the investigation in the Occurrence Book kept by every hulk.

Not many months later a pardon was granted to the clerk. Although it was stated to have been granted on medical grounds, the surgeon of the depôt declared that he had never recommended such a course, as he would have been called upon to do had the accustomed routine been carried out. By some means or other the pardon arrived; immediately there followed a great destruction of papers in Botham's office—Masterman afterwards asserted that he had been "squaring the accounts". It was late when he finished—past nine o'clock, when "Lights Out" had been sounded and all prisoners, except the crew of the gig which was waiting to take an Admiralty messenger ashore, were asleep. Into that gig with the Admiralty messenger went Botham, "in a manner that I never saw a prisoner go away before; he was concealed away from this ship", in a specially made civilian suit of clothes, after having served no more than three and a half years of his sentence. But though he had, rightly or wrongly, regained freedom, he had not thereby regained health; only a few weeks after his restoration to liberty, he died.

At about the same time there was also at Woolwich a convict named H. A. Styles. Styles had been a medical man, and soon became in the hospital ship *Unité* very much what Botham had made himself on board the *Warrior*. The surgeon at Woolwich during this period was (like most people connected with the hulks) a man neither very efficient nor very diligent, and his assistant, conscientious but unqualified, could rely but little upon the help of his superior. At first Styles seemed to him a godsend; in order to gain time for further study, he soon got into the habit of leaving far more to the prisoner than was in any circumstances justifiable. According to the system theoretically in force, convalescents on board the hospital ship were appointed (by sanction of the Medical Officer) night nurses to those whose cases were more serious; once Styles had secured practical command of the vessel, night nurses were chosen almost wholly from those who could not afford to pay him enough for escaping the duty—with the result that they were sometimes in a worse state than those they were supposed to be tending. Another of Styles' paths to power was in having control of medicines which ought properly to have been dispensed by the Assistant Medical Officer; in this way he gained access to a number of dangerous drugs, including laudanum, with which, if he had too much sense of responsibility to play fast and loose, he certainly bestowed occasional peace and pleasure on his friends, and wreaked vengeance on his enemies. He was also roundly accused by several of the latter of administering croton oil, a violent purgative, instead of the cod liver oil that had been prescribed.

Some ten years before Styles and Botham, in 1832, a Select Committee on Secondary Punishment had brought to

light so widespread a lack of discipline that we might well
wonder if any advance at all had been made in the Convict
Establishment since Capper's arrival—or, indeed, since its
earliest days. Among those who gave evidence before the
Committee was an ex-convict, referred to as A.B.; he had
been sentenced in 1826 to seven years' transportation for
being concerned in robbing a solicitor's office, but had
served his time (five years' actual imprisonment) in the
Retribution at Sheerness. This is his description of an
evening on board:

"You are allowed to converse along with your companions locked up with you, and you can sing or smoke or
talk or do anything of that sort till ten o'clock. There is
plenty of light to read by. There were free-and-easys
sometimes; perhaps a hundred all in one room, and mess
tables and forms on each side in every room; and then
there are large kettles of tea, and flash songs, singing till
ten or eleven o'clock at night, and dancing and fiddling;
there are two fiddles, what they play in the chapel with;
there is a clarionet and two fiddles, a violin and a bass, and
dancing and fiddling till ten or eleven o'clock, with hot tea
and smoking tobacco. You could not see before you,
hardly; you felt just as if you were intoxicated when you
were coming out, what with the tobacco and hot tea, and
one thing and the other. The officers seemed pleased at it;
sometimes they would come in and stop while they were
singing, and if a man could sing a good song perhaps they
would give him a shilling or sixpence."

Here is another story of discipline on board the
Retribution:

"Mr. Capper surprised us when he came down one
Christmas; there was a young man there who had had, I
think it was two pheasants sent down [by his friends] and
we had three or four of the tables joined together; and we

[113]

had a dozen or fourteen different kinds of meat, besides a fowl; and we had got a dozen of glasses, and some small beer poured into the glasses, and it looked more like wine than small beer; so Mr. Capper came, and he said, 'God bless me', says he, 'I hope spirits are not allowed here'. So the Second Mate came and tasted it; and then we all jumped up, and said we were making ourselves merry at the expense of our friends"—an explanation which apparently satisfied the zealous, intelligent, and humane Capper, since A.B.'s evidence is the first we hear of the incident.

Visitors, continued A.B., were allowed on board about once in three months. The prisoner seems to have been excused labour; "we could be together all day on the quarter-deck and have tea or anything". They could stop for a maximum of three days, since they had often travelled from remote parts of England, or even Scotland, but had been known to stop as long as a week. When women came, 'sometimes they are in the smoking cabin; if a female is respectable, sometimes, if she gives a shilling to the quarter-deck man, he lets her go into the smoking cabin; that is a little place where the officers smoke". There the couple are "quite in private". Any woman, said A.B., would be admitted to a prisoner on board "if she comes as his wife or sister".

Robbery from fellow convicts, selling Government stores, extortion from newcomers, gambling and coining appear to have been the favourite pastimes of those who were being reformed. As for the Overseer, he too had his amusement, if we are to believe the following extract from A.B.'s evidence:

"Have you any reason to think that part of the allowance made to you as a convict by Government was withheld from you?—No; but the Captain had a certain sum of money allowed from Government that would purchase very good beef by contract; but he contracts with a butcher in the town for a certain sum less, which causes the meat to be a good deal worse than it ought to be.

"You mean at a lower price?—Yes, but I shall tell you how he manages that; there is always about ten or a dozen pounds of good meat bought with the bad; sometimes more, half a quarter; this he will cause to be hung up, and the bad to be cooked, in case any gentleman comes down to the ship; and then he shows them this good meat, and tells them that is what the men have.

"How do you know this to be the case?—I have heard the Captain's clerk talking about it, and saying what a dreadful shame it was. I can mention one instance; there was some gentleman came down, and there was a beautiful piece of meat hanging up, and the Captain went to him, and showed him the meat, and he said 'My Lord' or 'Your Lordship' (he spoke very high), and gave him to understand that that was such meat as the prisoners had, and he expressed great satisfaction, and said it was very good beef; and he also showed him some bread that he had got, and the bread was pretty near white, and our bread is always very bad; you can just break it in two, and throw a bit against the wall, and it will stick like clay, and weigh so very heavy; and the beef is as thin; the ribs are not so thick as my two fingers; it is nothing but cow beef.

"Do you think any part of the clothes allowed by Government were withheld by the Captain?—I am sure they were; because I have seen it in the rules and orders of the house that every prisoner is allowed a suit of slops every six months, and that is a jacket, waistcoat, and breeches, and shirt, handkerchief, stockings, shoes; well, instead of that they will make you wear the shoes perhaps nine or twelve months, or perhaps fifteen; I have been eighteen months without a pair of new shoes; and perhaps when you want a jacket, you go to the officer of your deck, and you ask him for one, and he will give you an old one, free from holes, but still not a new one; and a shirt and handkerchief and stockings the same."

Evidence was also taken by the Committee from three other convicts lodged in Millbank Prison after varying periods spent in the hulks.

Mannister Wortz had been for seven months on board the *Leviathan* at Portsmouth. He described much the same sort of evening on board as A.B. had done, adding that "the officers would stand and listen and join in almost". Beer-drinking in the wards was habitual and apparently condoned; rum was sometimes smuggled from the dockyard with the help of free labourers. Friends, male or female, were allowed on board without any examination, so long as they were respectably dressed. Prisoners were not obliged, said Wortz, to wash every day—"sometimes we were not able to procure water below the deck; I knew several young prisoners who had not got anything in which they could get water, and they could not wash themselves in the morning". Besides, a "scarcely sufficient" allowance of soap was made, and no means of drying were provided.

On board the *York*, also at Portsmouth, according to the second witness, William Brett, prisoners were obliged to wash for Sunday musters, but not otherwise; they were allowed two pints of water and, every three weeks, two ounces of soap. In the evenings, fighting took place between decks, beer and occasionally spirits were drunk, and gambling was indulged in, all to the accompaniment of songs and uproar. Friends were allowed to remain for three or four days. When Brett was transferred to Chatham he found conditions rather better—"although we only got a pint of water there, they were more clean in general than at

Portsmouth. . . . They were a different sort of people at Chatham; there was more disturbance; they took greater advantage at Chatham than they did at Portsmouth; they seemed to be older thieves."

Thomas Knight, the third witness, spoke of his two months on board the *Ganymede* at Woolwich. No dancing or singing appears to have taken place during the evenings, but there was much "scuffling and knocking about". Gambling was common and pilfering incessant—"you can keep nothing, you have no place to keep anything in, and anything you take is left open to them; if you leave anything in your locker it is sure to be gone". As to cleanliness, "if a man did not want to wash himself he need not wash himself all the week except on Sundays", when, if found dirty, "he would be scrubbed". Although a strictly limited amount was permitted, "as much tobacco as we liked" was actually smoked.

On such evidence it is not surprising that the Committee drew up a report "expressing their unqualified disapprobation of the whole system pursued with respect to convicts on board the hulks"—which meant, of course, not that they disapproved of housing felons in hulks at all, but merely that they thought the hulks might be better managed. Indeed, they, like their honourable predecessors, were obsessed by the "advantageousness" of prison-ships:

"Notwithstanding all that your Committee have been under the necessity of stating, with respect to the system hitherto pursued in the hulks, they are by no means prepared to recommend the abolition of the Convict Establishment. The punishment of mere transportation to New South Wales . . . is not sufficient to deter from commission of crime, and as yet no means have been suggested of inflicting adequate punishment in the Penal Colonies without entailing a very great additional expense on the Country. It is therefore necessary that the more exclusively penal part of the sentence of criminals condemned to transportation should be inflicted before they are sent to New South Wales; but as the Penitentiary [Millbank] is not sufficiently large to receive, even for a limited period, all those who are sentenced to transportation, and is, besides, attended with a heavy expense, an improved system of hard labour in the Dockyards and Arsenals, which may repay to the Country a portion of the cost of maintaining the convicts, appears to your Committee desirable; and they entertain a confident expectation that, with judicious management, such labour may be made effectual to the punishment of the criminal, and conducive to his moral improvement."

Whereupon the Committee proceeded to recommend a stricter separation of prisoners by night; yet "as the Committee find that such separation on board the convict ships is impracticable, it will be necessary to construct places of confinement on shore, as nearly as possible on the plan of those in the United States, which appear to leave nothing to be desired on the score of economy or usefulness". Out of that recommendation arose the "model" prison at Pentonville; but at the same time, it seems to have left the hulks very much as they had previously been. Other recommendations—such as prohibiting visits from friends, cutting off permission to buy tobacco, and prolonging hours of labour—to a certain extent tightened up the whole system for a few years; but very soon slackness once more made itself felt, and the next bracing it received proved final.

Interior of a civil hulk, 1846
Top: A Gallery
Below: Convict Ward

Interior of a civil hulk, 1846
Top: Wash-house
Below: Chapel

Chapter Thirteen

"HELL UPON EARTH"

THE cutting off of luxuries and the lengthening of hours of labour, as recommended by the Committee of 1832, produced a minor revolution in life on board the hulks; yet the state of affairs below decks at night, though changed, could show scarcely any real improvement. For one evil had been substituted another.

In 1835 there was appointed a Committee of the House of Lords "to inquire into the present state of the several Gaols and Houses of Correction in England and Wales"; the most interesting sections of its report summarise the evidence given by seventeen convicts, then in Millbank, who had served the first part of their sentence in the hulks.

One witness, a lad twenty years old, from Carmarthen, had been put on board the *Discovery* at Deptford. "He was in the upper deck, where there were a great many prisoners, probably not less than 100; they all slept together in the same division, in hammocks, as close as they could be stowed; there were old prisoners appointed as watchmen, who sat up, had a light burning, and relieved each other every two hours; the watch was not set until 10 o'clock; from dark up to that hour they did as they pleased; there was singing, but not in a loud voice, cursing and swearing, and obscene talk; thinks it is impossible for anyone to be on board the hulks even for a few days without contamination."

Several points deserve to be emphasised in this account. In the first place, the *Discovery* (which, it may be recalled, was of only 300 tons) was not divided into the wards common in all the larger hulks—and most of the smaller ones as well. Her flat decks, moreover, appear to have been seriously overcrowded—yet not so seriously as in the *Justitia*, where, according to another convict, "there were three tiers of hammocks, one over the other" in each division; or as in the *Ganymede*, where the hammocks were also in tiers. In the *Ganymede*, as on board the *Discovery*, "all sorts of iniquity was carried on, robbing each other, quarrelling and fighting, cursing and swearing, and singing of bawdy songs; the language was most horrid to listen to . . . there was gambling carried on, card-playing, dominoes, and pitch-and-toss". Another witness, rather more discriminating in his description of the *Ganymede* (which lodged roughly 350 prisoners), said that "the conversation among so many persons was of all kinds, some talked decently and properly, some talked of their trials and former convictions, some of them wished to be sent abroad, some cursed and swore, many talked profanely or indecently". However generously they might be portrayed, in short, evil communications seem to have corrupted almost every hulk—on board the *Leviathan* "there was very bad conversation carried on, cursing and swearing often, with histories of former exploits"; on board the *Retribution* "crime was the constant subject of talk, and that after this they would never go to work again; must go thieving; intended to do it; wished to do it". Only the *York* at Gosport is singled out as being comparatively free from obscenity.

Both the witness from Carmarthen and nearly all his

fellow witnesses spoke highly of the watchmen, or wardsmen, who acted as section leaders, as it were, in each deck.
Thus on board the *Fortitude* at Chatham, the wardsman of
the class from which a witness came "was very strict and
kept good order and regularity in his division, and was not
in the slightest fear of any of them; when they attempted
to talk or sing improperly he immediately put a stop to it;
no robbery was committed in that division, nor any gaming
permitted". In the *Justitia* "there was a gangsman or
wardsman to 16 prisoners, and they maintained good order
and decency among the rest, set them a good example". In
the *York*, the wardsman of the witness's class "was a quiet
decent man, who did all he could to maintain regularity,
prevented smoking, which, although prohibited, often
took place". The one vessel specifically mentioned as
having no wardsmen at night was the *Ganymede*, where a
lantern, supposed to be left burning, was often blown out,
so that prisoners could the more easily rob each other.
The *Ganymede* appears to have been Pandemonium, and
we are not surprised when one witness speaks of it as
"hell upon earth".

Yet, from almost whatever hulk witnesses came, the
phrase "hell upon earth", or something very like it, finds
its way into their evidence. One "freely admits that if it
should be his son's fate to be placed in confinement, he
prays to God that he may never be put into a hulk".
Another asserted that "whatever little remains of innocence
or honesty a man might have is sure to be lost there; the
longer a man remains there, the worse he becomes; they
would ruin a man for ever". A third declared that "he
must contract habits of idleness and wickedness of all sorts,
and would never hold up his head again as an honest man".
While as for a fourth, he "would sooner pass the whole of
his life in the Penitentiary, or even in the strictest state

of solitude, than be placed either in the hulks or in Newgate".

An ex-convict who gave evidence before the Committee was Thomas Dexter. Born at Kettering, in Northamptonshire, he had lost both parents in infancy and been reared by his grandfather. When he began to grow up, and in consequence of family quarrels, he went to Wellingborough and entered into contract with a man to teach him shoemaking; the contract at an end, he set up for himself, married, and opened an evening school, which continued for some years. Trade declined, however, and Dexter was forced to close his little business, making a living instead by selling shoes on commission in London. London too failing him, he turned porter; then, "under circumstances of distress" in 1828, he stole a pair of shoes, valued at three shillings, for which he was sentenced at the Old Bailey to seven years' transportation. He was sent to Newgate for some months; but at last orders were received to remove him and two dozen others to the *Dolphin* at Chatham.

A few days after his arrival on board it was discovered that he was a shoemaker. Since shoemakers appear to have been scarce in the Convict Establishment at that time, he was very soon transferred to the *Canada* hospital ship, and later to the *Cumberland*, to work at his accustomed trade.

"Was the language in the *Dolphin* hulk much better than what you had heard at Newgate?—Not at all, unless it was in the presence of the guard, but when the prisoners were by themselves I should say the language was quite as bad as at Newgate.

"Do you think a man would learn much good in the hulks?—I am sure he could not, among his fellow prisoners."

Speaking of the practice of pardoning men for good

behaviour, Dexter (who was himself pardoned in 1833) stated that "I have known it to be the case, that by putting a sovereign in the hand of the Captain's clerk the name has been put down in the list sent to the Secretary of State, and the prisoner has got away one quarter of a year sooner than he would have done if the list had gone on in the usual course; that I can speak to positively; that was in the early part of my imprisonment; I have known it to be done in more than one instance; it was different from that before I came away".

It was Dexter's strong opinion that men must leave their hulk "much worse than they went to it". As for the special hulk for boys, the *Euryalus* at Chatham, "frequently when I have seen it in a newspaper that a Judge has sentenced a boy out of mercy to him to the hulks, I have made the observation that was it a child of mine I would rather see him dead at my feet than see him sent to that place".

Dexter could speak with some experience of the juvenile convicts, since for two years he was employed as nurse at their hospital. His account of it will serve aptly as prelude to the chapter devoted later to the *Euryalus*.

"When these boys were ill in the convict hospital, did you see any signs of their being sensible of the offences which they had committed?—In very few instances. . . .

"Did many of them die when you were in that hospital?—Many. . . .

"What was the oldest boy that you recollect in that hospital?—Seventeen.

"And the youngest?—Six years and seven months.

"Do you know what he was convicted of?—I understood for some robbery at Birmingham, from the Warwick Assizes; and the Judge asked his mother if she would take him home again provided a lenient sentence was passed, and she refused to do it; he was consequently sentenced to transportation, that he might be taken care of; that was the general report.

"Was that boy reformed?—He died very shortly after he came in; and he was so young that he had hardly any religious or moral impressions upon his mind."

From this rapid survey, based upon the evidence of prisoners themselves, we can perhaps form a truer estimate of the state of affairs in the hulks than from all Capper's sleek reports and the assurances of people in authority that, although things might not at the moment be quite at their best, yet there was nothing inherently wrong with the system, which, indeed, must be considered both reformatory and economical. But is there no one to whom we can turn for confirmation of our estimate, no one of unimpeachable prestige upon whom we can rely both for the facts and for their implications? From the arrival of Capper until roughly 1835, the chaplains appointed to each hulk had had matters, so to speak, all their own way.

What have they to tell us?

Chapter Fourteen

PRISONERS' SOULS

TO no one but a Government official would the notion occur of making a chaplain present every six months a report on the moral state of his flock—to declare, as it were, how many virtuous rabbits he had been able to produce in that period out of a singularly empty hat. Yet that was what the Chaplains of the hulks were expected to do; and ridiculous as the practice may have been when measured by any kind of spiritual standard, it does give us, at this distance of time, an opportunity of becoming acquainted with them to a degree which would otherwise have been impossible.

We have already caught glimpses of the early provision for religious guidance on board the hulks, when at first they were dependent upon voluntary charity and later when one chaplain had to serve a whole depôt. After 1812 every ship had its own chaplain; on board, his stature grew with the years until he seems to have wielded an influence second only to that of the Overseer.

In the 1830s one of the better among the hulk chaplains wrote an account of the manner in which he spent his time:

"I frequently go down to one of the decks about 7 o'clock in the morning, to witness who do and who do not attend prayers. After breakfast, my forenoons are occupied in composing appropriate discourses, etc., for the ensuing Sunday. Some of my hearers are very ignorant as well as obdurate; to produce any good in these, the adoption of very plain and strong language seems to be not only judicious but indispensable. Others of my hearers, though they be very degenerate in principles, are critical, and would be glad of opportunities to ridicule what they had heard, to the hardening of their fellow prisoners who are ignorant; hence a diction somewhat correct is necessary. The reading of the same discourses over again would not keep their attention equally alive as the delivery of those recently composed doth. To transcribe discourses, however good and appropriate, would allow them, who, although they are convicts, have been readers and remember, room to reflect. Feeling the weight of these considerations, much of my time is occupied in the composition of sermons.

"My afternoons are open for any prisoner who may want my advice or reproof. About 5 in the evening the school opens; I attend, and render that assistance which to me appears expedient and necessary. At 7 the chapel doors are opened for the admission of them who are desirous of attending the prayers which are offered up at the closing of the school. I very frequently engage. At other times one of the teachers, whom I name, reads a printed form of prayer appointed for the evening, in a selection which I have recommended and purchased for that purpose. After this, between the hours of 8 and 11, I now and then go between decks, and if I see or hear anything amiss or tending to immoralise, I instantly administer reproof and report the offender or offenders to the Commanding Officer, whom I always find ready and active to co-operate in the promotion of virtue and in checking vice. On Sundays I generally read prayers and preach twice. After the second lesson in the evening service, I hear as many of the prisoners as are willing repeating the Church Catechism or the Articles of Religion. At this time I have opportunities to make some concise and pithy remarks, which (I hope) are felt at the time, and will be by some of them remembered to their real advantage."

As contrast may be mentioned the Rev. William Quarterman, who gave evidence before the Committee of 1835. Quarterman was Chaplain on board the *Ganymede*; but attached to the *Ganymede* at this time was a small vessel, the *Leven*, housing only about 120 prisoners who were, for most routine purposes, included in the returns of the larger ship. Sunday service, attended by the men of both hulks, was held in a shed on shore; and Quarterman stated that he was in the habit of visiting the *Ganymede* two or three times a week. He considered, he added, the *Ganymede* and *Leven* as one; when pressed on the point, he admitted that he did not go on board the *Leven* at all, that the men in her had no religious instruction, and that in both vessels "I do not hold intercourse with the prisoners".

For this, Quarterman was paid £100 a year (he held also an appointment on shore); but, like our more conscientious informant, he did keep an eye upon the evening school held on board. The first school had been formed in 1813 in the *Captivity* at Portsmouth, but did not last long; in 1829, when the Rev. James Inman was urging the formation of one in the *Hardy* at Tipnor, he wrote of the prisoners that "their leisure hours after public labour have been spent in a great measure very usefully, in mutually instructing each other in reading, writing, and manufacturing small articles for their own advantage, such as list shoes, small baskets from the rushes growing near the ship, etc., the latter part of such employment in extra hours has very lately been stopped; and I am sorry that reasons should exist for giving an order to this effect".

In most ships, however, schools had been formed before this. It was only later that one of the guards acted as schoolmaster, or a separate schoolmaster was appointed. At first, a convict of tolerable education was told off by the Chaplain to instruct such of his fellows as wished to make the best use of their time; for attendance at the school was voluntary. During the late 'teens and early twenties of the century we come across many requests for "elementary books", "slates and copybooks", and similar apparatus; and that emphasis should be placed on the elementary nature of the matter provided is shown in a return made by the Rev. Joseph Garton, of the *Stirling Castle*, Devonport, in 1840.

"The number of convicts examined", he said, "is 331. Of these, 157 have been educated in common day schools, a few, six or seven, in common boarding schools; 103 in National and other Free Schools (about 90 in National Schools); 80 have never been to any school, and one, whose friends move in the higher ranks of society, has received a liberal education. Again, 162 can read and write, some imperfectly; 89 can read but cannot write; 80 can neither read nor write."

In 1854 there were 52 prisoners on board the *Defence* at Woolwich who could not read, of whom 16 learned in the course of a year to "read imperfectly". It is perhaps scarcely to be expected that, after a day's hard labour at stacking timber or scraping shot, men should be able to throw off weariness and turn their minds to the unaccustomed task of absorbing knowledge. Easy reading and writing, and (in accordance with the current ideas of reformation) religious instruction generally, comprised all they had a chance of learning. Arithmetic was not encouraged; yet occasionally, one imagines, it was too hard for their simple intelligences, since all sorts of inducements had at various times to be offered in order to keep some of the schools alive. We may therefore cast a certain doubt upon the Chaplain who declared that "the willingness to receive instruction and the general aptitude which they [the prisoners] manifest are far beyond what I had expected from persons of their former habits"; and we may also take leave to regard with some caution the Chaplain who roundly asserted that "no institution was ever formed more likely to be useful in reclaiming the misguided than a school conducted on the principles with which it is carried on in this ship". Yet it is certain that, with all their faults, the evening schools were among the few redeeming features of the hulks, and that the time the Chaplains spent in them was, on the whole, the least likely to be wasted.

In 1815 the Rev. Thomas Price of the *Retribution* wrote: "I am of the opinion that it would be of essential service to them [the prisoners] if a library were established in the ship. . . . I would take charge of the books myself, keep an account to whom they were lent, and see that they were regularly and properly returned; for I consider nothing a trouble I can do for the benefit of these poor outcasts."

From this germ of an idea grew another institution which might have been no less beneficial than the evening schools. Here, perhaps, it is definitely unfortunate that Chaplains were so consistently prominent. The Rev. George Harker, of the *Dolphin*, reported in 1827 that "a small selection of the best religious publications has been made for the use of the men during their hours of relaxation from labour"; and when, a year or two afterwards, the Rev. William Tate wrote from Portsmouth that "a library of above 100 volumes has been collected in the *Leviathan*, of which the better characters are permitted to have free use", we have little difficulty in visualising the type of book which that library probably contained. It was all very well for the Rev. John

Adams to write from the *Stirling Castle* in 1842, that "if we can inspire a fondness for reading a great step will have been gained towards reclaiming the prisoners from habits of vice"; they needed a very different selection of matter from that which the Chaplains thrust upon them. In 1848 the Rev. Stewart Hanna, at Woolwich, flattered himself that "my experience is now sufficient to teach me the sort of article which might at once be useful in itself and likely to meet with a ready demand among the prisoners"; six or seven years later, the library of the *Defence* at Woolwich, which comprised more than a thousand volumes, included such apparently inappropriate works as Marcel's *Conversations on Natural Philosophy*, Paley's *Moral Philosophy*, *The Pursuit of Knowledge under Difficulties* (ironic title!), *The Rites and Worship of the Jews*, and *First Sundays at Church*. Books, says a contemporary author, "teaching kindly lessons in the homely incidents of life, which all may read and comprehend, are hardly to be found upon the Chaplain's library shelf". The Chaplain, he was told, had objected to the inclusion of Dickens' *Household Words*.

Price must have grown more or less hardened to watching his good ideas mishandled by those in authority. We have seen him proposing the division of the hulks into cells; but inefficient discipline robbed the plan of its full advantage. His scheme for ships' libraries went astray through narrow professionalism and lack of sympathetic insight. He was the first to agitate for a hulk for boys; when after several years the *Euryalus* was established, and he was appointed Chaplain, he demanded too high a standard and too keen a devotion to duty from the officers, quarrelled with them, and was transferred elsewhere with an official snub. Price was by no means free from the errors and delusions of his cloth; but he went far towards redeeming them by an urgency in the cause of humanity of which few, if any, of his colleagues, and none of superiors, were capable.

Take, for instance, the Rev. Edward Edwards, who spent the greater part of his working life in the Convict Establishment. "Upwards of 60 men and boys", he wrote in 1817, "repeat once a month the Church Catechism; about 20 repeat memoriter the Thirty Nine Articles". In 1818, "once a month, about 25 of them repeat memoriter the Thirty Nine Articles of Religion; once a week we generally have a Homily (and sometimes two or three) repeated memoriter. . . . Hugh Farrol (who, according to report, was a most wild and depraved lad) thus repeated last evening the Homily against the fears of death, with very considerable pathos and propriety. The conduct of this boy is now exemplary good." In 1819, "religious improvement appears to be on the increase. During the year now closing, 419 Chapters of Holy Scriptures, 48 Epistles, and as many Gospels are partitioned in the morning services of respective Sundays; and two-and-twenty Homilies have been repeated memoriter. . . . Two hundred and four repeat the Catechism and 65 the Articles of Religion once a month." In 1820, "one thousand chapters (averaging 25 verses) of Holy Writ, 48 Epistles and Gospels, and 15 Homilies have been committed to memory and rehearsed in the chapel during the last year; 192 are in the habit of rehearsing monthly the Church Catechism and 48 the Church Articles of Religion". In 1821, "two hundred and eighty Chapters of Holy Writ containing 7750 verses, and 4 Homilies, have been repeated memoriter during the last half year".

What feats of memory—and what futility! Surely, if ever men were saved through the instrumentality of statistics, they were the unhappy flock of the Rev. Edward

Edwards. Yet we must hesitate before singling him out for condemnation, for most of the other Chaplains were from time to time (and a few nearly permanently) subject to an almost incredible self-delusion—if self-delusion it was. Listen, for instance, to Price himself in 1818:

"I am aware that an unfavourable opinion prevails with many persons respecting the real state of the hulks; nor am I a stranger to the dreadful apprehensions that some prisoners entertain on being sent to them; but I find the very same persons have, upon their arrival here, expressed in unqualified terms their agreeable surprise, and that the present management of the ship afforded them such comfort and ease as surpassed everything they experienced in prison, and were glad of the change."

"Nothing", declared the Rev. William Prowse, who was transferred to the *Dolphin* in 1828, "is omitted which can be done for the good of the prisoners"; the Rev. Samuel Watson, of the *Justitia*, paid tribute to the "sound, clean and well ventilated vessel", which, he continues, will provide a remedy "appropriate and efficacious, such as will afford culprits the best opportunity of being preserved in health, and of regaining habits of industry and honesty, and such as in the meantime may enable them to make to the country the best atonement in their power for offences against her laws, by the labour of their hands, at the least possible expense for their custody and maintenance". Tate says that "as much regard is paid to the personal comfort of the convicts as is consistent with the object of their being sent hither; their treatment is humane; their wards clean and airy, and their food wholesome". Tate also spoke of "a great appearance of a progressive movement continuing to take place among them". Prowse averred that "among many of them I have reason to believe that a real work of moral reformation is in progress".

Price declared that "when the general character of the prisoners is considered, with relation to their former abandoned associations, in a long and habitual course of sin, now to behold them modest, tractable, quiet, and regardful of instruction, is a manifestation that this alteration can only be attributable to mild discipline and the power of religion". The Rev. H. J. Dawes (Price's successor in the *Euryalus*) had the impudence to assert that "it must be gratifying to a humane mind to know that the unfortunate youths who are imprisoned in this ship are enjoying the blessing of a moral and religious education", and in other reports speaks in quite extravagant terms of his own success.

Nor does the statistical Edwards fall below our expectations. "I never anticipated that my poor labours would ever produce half the good effects, which they appear to have done." A little later, "the practice of morality and good conduct in our ship is still advancing. Were I to particularise, and you had not been there, you would perhaps be somewhat inclined to view my statement as hyperbolical. As you are furnished with information from others on the subject, to enlarge is unnecessary. If it could be proper to adopt a phrase in common use with reference to my profession, I would truly say, I take a pride in my business; with respect to my success therein, verity compels me to say, I am indebted to steady, active, and prompt co-operation from the Captain."

Self-delusion it may have been; Quarterman suggests another interpretation by taking a much more direct line of attack. "I cannot", he says, "express myself in terms sufficiently strong as would convey to a stranger the correct idea of the high state of discipline to which the convicts on board the *Warrior* [at Woolwich] have, through your instrumentality, been brought. From your frequent visits amongst us, you are fully aware of the state they are in; but I consider it my duty to bear testimony to your indefatigable exertions on behalf of the service, and have much pleasure in congratulating you that you have been spared to see your labours crowned with success."

It was, in short, just as well for the Chaplain to remember on which side his bread was buttered, even though most of the acknowledgement had, from professional tact, to be made to the Deity.

Nor is our estimate of Chaplains enhanced when we read some of their references to the men whose spiritual welfare had been entrusted to them. When we are told, for instance (as we are told by the Rev. David Jones, of the *Discovery* at Deptford) that the conduct of the prisoners has been "good and in every way becoming their degraded station"; or when the Rev. Henry Wynter writes that "the convicts on board the *Cumberland* and *Canada* continue to behave orderly and submissive (with a few exceptions), suited to their humiliating condition"; then, even allowing for the Evangelical phraseology of the 1820s it appears possible that the speaker was unduly conscious of his own moral rectitude. When cholera broke out in 1832, the Chaplain at Woolwich, the Rev. Samuel Watson, refused to bury the dead until at least half a dozen were awaiting interment— and then, instead of accompanying them to the graveside, he read the funeral service from the deck of the hulk (which was a mile away), and let drop his handkerchief when he reached the committal sentences, as a sign to the officer on shore to lower the bodies to their last resting place.

As congregations compelled to listen to his sermons, prisoners receive encomiums from almost every Chaplain. Says Edwards: "A beneficed clergyman of this neighbourhood officiated last Sunday in my stead; after he had done, and retired, he said, 'Well, I am astonished! I do not think that there is in all England a congregation who conduct themselves during Divine Worship so orderly and apparently so devout as yours do'." Tate avers that "at evening prayers (which are regularly read in each division by the convicts themselves) they are orderly and decorous; at chapel services serious and attentive; at the communion solemn and devout". Price calls them "remarkably attentive at chapel, and appear to value the privilege of hearing that Word 'which is able to make them wise unto salvation' ". In hospitals too, the sick "seem thankful for the Chaplain's attentions, and those especially whose diseases were of an alarming description exhibited the most consolatory marks of contrition and of apparently true penitence". At another time, "those few whose cases terminated fatally exhibited the most satisfactory signs of true penitence". Again, "it is consoling to be able to state that, with scarcely a single exception, the sufferers exhibited the most satisfactory signs of genuine contrition and real repentance". During the cholera epidemic of 1832, those from the *Ganymede* and *Discovery* "evinced a becoming fortitude and resignation under the fatal disease with which it has pleased the Almighty so lately to afflict them"; at Chatham, "I should observe that during the raging of the pestilence there were among the convicts some affecting instances of contrition; and while I cannot but lament the transition of so many into eternity with scarcely time for reflection, I am glad to find any receiving the warning so as to consider their latter end". As for Watson, he is "inclined to believe that the alarm itself has been of good effect, having had fewer occasions for remonstrance or reprimand during the last quarter than in several preceding"—that from the man who was himself so alarmed that he scamped one of the most fundamental of his duties!

Until roughly 1835 Chaplains had the run of the hospital

ships, and it is interesting to turn to their comments on the places in which so many "satisfactory" deaths occurred. Thus we find reference to "the perfect state of the new hospital ship"; while Watson opines that "the hospital is in the best condition, so that I think every patient who is not callous to common feeling would unite with us in blessing God for the provision there afforded". Quotations in the same sense could be continued, were it necessary to do so. After 1835, however, the supremacy of the Chaplain begins to show definite signs of waning; not long afterwards it is the surgeon who assumes a more vigorous importance than formerly. One cannot help wondering whether there was any connection between the two tendencies.

Chapter Fifteen

PRISONERS' BODIES

INSTEAD of blessing God for the provision afforded on board the various hospital ships, prisoners might have taken the name of the Deity less in vain, had they blessed Him for sparing them from the many epidemics which swept over the hulks.

Capper's six-monthly reports, of course, always put the best face upon these outbreaks. Dysentery which invaded the hulks at Woolwich in 1816 "was not confined to the convicts alone, the military and the inhabitants having also been violently attacked with it". Two years later, smallpox (from which, on the assurance of the Rev. Samuel Watson, the prisoners "had been providentially preserved for twenty years at least") caused, according to Capper, the loss of only four convicts. In 1821 typhus broke out, again at Woolwich, though "without materially adding to the deaths at that depôt"; when it broke out at Portsmouth five years later, there was "considerably less mortality than was contemplated". For two years after 1821 the ships were normally healthy; then, "an indication of scurvy in a rather formidable shape" appeared in two of them; it was "subdued without the loss of one prisoner". In 1826, when the Woolwich and Chatham depôts were attacked by inflammation of the lungs, "in the majority of cases where death ensued, it appeared from the surgeons that there had been previous existing disease". In the following year "severe sickness which terminated fatally in several cases", and which spread from Woolwich to Portsmouth, was attributed to "the severe and unsettled weather". Influenza at Devonport and Gosport in 1831 was "subdued without any fatal consequences"; and an outbreak of erysipelas at Woolwich, in 1846, Capper did not mention at all.

But an occasion which he could not pass over so airily was the first epidemic of cholera in 1832; it was, he had to admit, "attended with much loss of life", though he added that "the proportion of deaths compared with the number of cases has been far less than the average in society at large who have been attacked with that disorder"—for the outbreak, originating in Central Asia, had swept first across Russia, and then over a great part of Europe, reaching even the United States and Canada and giving rise everywhere to a heavy mortality. From the hulks at Woolwich it spread, in 1833, to those at Portsmouth, where also "the deaths consequent upon this singular and fatal disease have been numerous during the year". For sixteen years it vanished; but in 1848—the year following Capper's retirement—it returned, killing more than 53,000 persons in England and Wales and taking heavy toll from the occupants of the hulks in every depôt.

This second epidemic was curiously capricious in its lodging. At Woolwich, the *Justitia* and the *Unité* hospital ship were attacked; the *Warrior*, moored only a short distance away, was immune, and remained so throughout. That the entire depôt did not suffer more greatly was attributed by Capper's successor, Herbert Voules, to the devotion of G. H. Dabbs, the Senior Medical Officer, who "resided on board the hospital ship and never left the vessel, except on duty, during the period of the visitation".

[138]

At Portsmouth, whither it very soon spread, first the *York*, then the *Stirling Castle*, were involved, as well as prisoners, guards and even one of the surgeons; it "assumed a character of intensity and malignity such as it had not before exhibited", and nearly 50 per cent of the patients fell victims to its ravages.

Six years later, in 1854 (and as part of an epidemic which cost the country 20,000 lives), it returned once again to Woolwich; but either it was not so virulent or hospital arrangements had improved, for rather less than one-third of the cases ended in the death of the patient.

It is a pity that no comprehensive statistics appear to exist from which to tell the annual death-rate on board the hulks throughout Capper's régime. We have already seen that, during the last quarter of the previous century, roughly one in three of the prisoners died. For the first forty years of the nineteenth we can form no reliable estimate; but in 1841, out of 638 prisoners in the *Warrior*, although there were 400 admissions to hospital, there were only 39 deaths—about 6 per cent of the total number on board. If the *Warrior* may be regarded as typical of all the hulks in this respect (though in certain others she was superior to them), the improvement is noteworthy. At the same time, the hulks were always, and by their very nature, unhealthy—catarrh, scurvy, scrofula, diarrhoea or lung complaints might almost always be found in them, and apparently ineradicable vermin rendered both them and the hospital ships far from sanitary. Sometimes, when the convicts' shirts were hanging out to dry, they would, in the words of one of the guards, give the impression of having been sprinkled over with pepper. Once an Overseer determined to rid his vessel of this third plague by pressing the convicts' clothing with a hot iron; but when, almost immediately after each application, the face of the iron became covered with an appearance of red rust, he gave up the attempt in despair. So far as can be discovered, most of the Overseers agreed to accept the inevitable and not waste time, energy, and the taxpayers' money in efforts at altering it.

Conditions like these scarcely seem to call for any special thankfulness towards the Almighty. After about 1840 admissions to hospital were made more numerous by the enforcement of a new regulation transporting to the Australian settlements a proportion of able-bodied men direct from Millbank, thus tending to reserve the hulks for weaklings—making them, in short, a kind of convalescent depôt for men destined to serve at home either the whole of their sentences or a longer period than the usual. In a report dated 1845 Capper says:

"A number of these prisoners have so far benefited by change of air, diet, and exercise not at first amounting to labour, that they have been sufficiently restored to health in a few months to enable them to undergo their sentences of transportation, which have consequently been carried into effect. And although the deaths among this class of prisoner have not at present been very much above the usual average, yet as the numbers of diseased convicts are rapidly accumulating on board the hulks from the cause above-mentioned, it cannot be concealed that an increased mortality will henceforth occur among a comparatively small body of prisoners."

All this threw much work on the surgeons, and even if they had been better men than they actually were, they could not probably have effected great improvement. But they too, or some of them, suffered from the slackness that pervaded the whole Convict Establishment, and were occasionally (though rarely, it must be admitted) given to outbursts of optimism directed towards the Superintendent rather than warranted by facts. For the most part, however, in spite of their shortcomings they brought a challenge to bear upon Capper's management and must at times have sorely damaged his self-satisfaction.

Long before the cholera epidemic of 1848, the position of the hulks in the river at Woolwich had been criticised by Peter Bossy, who was at first surgeon to the *Warrior* and later became Senior Medical Officer of the depôt. The *Warrior*, he pointed out, floated only at high tide, and was actually resting on a mudbank for about ten hours out of the twenty-four. He did not view very seriously the refuse deposited during those hours, because he claimed that it was soon carried away by the stream. Near by were the marshes, which in his opinion were more important, since they were "capable of producing fever"; and there was also a pond which the tide seems to have reached during the winter but left stagnant throughout the summer. A few years later, when trying to account for cholera in the *Justitia*, Dabbs too criticised the nearness of the marshes, and also the fact that the *Justitia* was left dry for some time by the receding tide. Then, somewhat naively, he added: "There is also a drain both ahead and astern, which I suspect gave some intensity to the causes operating to produce disease. It may perhaps appear frivolous to assign much weight to these latter causes, yet when it is recollected the greater proportion of the cases of cholera took place amongst those on the landward side, and that every effect must have a cause, I know not otherwise how to account for the circumstances alluded to."

There was surely another operating cause, which Bossy mentions, not in connection with cholera, but in discussing the tuberculosis always to be found in the hulks—though not always under its proper name. "The ventilation and cleanliness of the classes", he says, "the hold, and every part of the ships; the diet, the clothing, the employment, and the general discipline to which they were subjected, were in all respects equal to, if not superior to, that of former years; care had been taken at an early period to protect them against cold and rain by extra clothing; fires were continually kept in the passages in every deck and in the hold, washing the classes had been entirely abandoned; yet catarrhs became numerous, and in many so serious that I could only conclude that the natural and constant depression of strength and spirits, which is ever experienced by those who are subjected to the hard labour and rigorous discipline of the hulks, was in these men so much heightened by the severity of the weather that they could not hold up against it."

It was all very well to blame the season; other, and more easily remediable matters might first have been regulated with propriety. Yet it must be repeated that Bossy and his colleagues were making some effort, even if only in self-justification, to improve first one aspect of the hulks, then another. They had attacked the position of the ships; they attacked also the dietary. Bossy says:

"A very great alteration in the nutritious properties of the diet would be accomplished if a superior quality of bread could be issued in lieu of the inferior now supplied, which contains a large proportion of bran, and which has a tendency to produce diarrhoea; it is almost wholly made from middlings, is often mixed with rye or damaged flour, and is soon sour. The brown bread is now the mainstay of the prisoner, and even a slight adulteration is felt as a considerable loss; its improvement would therefore be an essential advantage."

And again:

"For several years past I have observed a gradual increase in the number and severity of the cases of scurvy. I believe it to originate in the poorness and sameness of the diet adopted for the prisoners, and to have been much promoted by those regulations which deprived prisoners of all extraneous supplies of food while in prison, and of comforts in the hulks."

In these strictures he was supported by John Williams, of the *Briton* hospital ship at Portsmouth. Scurvy and scrofula, says Williams, "I cannot help attributing to the very small quantity of green vegetable matter allowed in the dietary. . . . I should feel desirous of urging a diminution of the oatmeal, and substitution of some other kind of food for breakfast; I have a strong impression that scrofula, if not produced, is much aggravated by an oatmeal diet. . . . And I would suggest that no prisoner, either old or young, be punished by deprivation of food, except by the authority of the Medical Officer."

At Portsmouth, the surgeon of the *Stirling Castle*, John Erskine Risk, pleaded for better clothing. "I would recommend for convicts in general flannel waistcoats with sleeves to be worn next to the skin, in preference to Guernsey frocks now in use outside the shirt; in fact, warm clothing, nutritious diet, exercise in the open air during the day, and dry well ventilated apartments at night will most naturally assist in preventing the development of scrofula, while without all and each of these being attended to, no medical treatment, however otherwise judicious, can succeed with convicts who have been confined for any considerable length of time on board the hulks."

The surgeon of the *Wye* hospital ship at Chatham, Archibald Robertson, however, attributed the high rate of disease at that depôt to more remote causes. "Though the number of prisoners", he wrote, "who have applied for medical assistance has been very great, the causes of their diseases (generally speaking) are not to be attributed to the circumstances under which they are placed in this Establishment; neither the general economy of the prison, the diet, the labour, nor the clothing, could have produced them. On the contrary, the remote and exciting causes are to be found in the previous prison discipline, solitary confinement, and low diet of the majority of our gaols, and which render very many of the convicts more fit for an hospital than for dockyard labour."

Besides weaklings in plenty, the hulks contained some whose cases were hopeless—the feeble-minded and insane. No differentiation appears to have been made between them and the rest of the convicts, unless they were definitely violent in character. Those who were tractable but simple received their full share of the lash—what effect it sometimes had upon them may be imagined. When they succeeded in committing suicide, it was written down an accident; unsuccessful attempts were rewarded either with solitary confinement upon bread and water, or with further floggings. Only when they became completely unmanageable were they sent to Bethlehem Hospital, or even, occasionally, transported. Bossy afterwards explained that he kept them on board as long as possible because he was certain that their lot would only be worse elsewhere.

It is of curious interest to watch the surgeons emulating the parsons in roseate addresses to Capper. Says Bossy, for instance:

"The provisions are excellent in quality and sufficient in quantity. The disposition of the wards and classes, and the perfect adaptation of every part of the hulk to the purposes required, render the state of the vessel satisfactory. The hospital ship is airy, clean, roomy, and well suited for the recovery and quietness of the patients." While John Brown, of Deptford, avers that "the vessel is kept in a state of perfect cleanliness, the decks are freely ventilated, the food and drink are good in quality; to all prisoners when ill the greatest attention is paid; everything is done, with

the view of curing their diseases, that the best efforts of
the healing art can effect".

To continue quotation, however, would only be to show
how much better were the parsons at this method of
approach. Surgeons, even when they were not honester
men, had been trained in a critical school and were more
accustomed to looking facts in the face. Their relative
optimism, no doubt, sprang, like that of the parsons, from
the necessity of justifying themselves before authority;
how very little it was warranted by the facts we shall see
when we come to the Inquiry of 1847—which was in part
at least due to allegations against the conduct of Bossy.

Chapter Sixteen

YOUNG VILLAINS

IN 1810 a shop-boy, Samuel Oliver, was convicted at the Old Bailey of the theft of two shillings from his master. This is how the Recorder passed sentence:

"Samuel Oliver, you have been tried by a jury of your country, and found guilty of one of the very worst descriptions of theft. You ungratefully betrayed the trust reposed in you by your employer, who paid you to be faithful to him. It is greatly to be lamented that young men, by so mean an offence, should bring themselves into the shameful situation in which you are now placed; and that there is a necessity of proceeding with rigour against a person who had apparently preserved a good character; but yours is a crime which the courts are determined never to treat with lenity. It is in itself hostile to every idea of domestic security. It is so harsh a violation of the confidence reposed, and of every bond of civil society, that, whenever it is proved, it cannot be punished with too much severity. The sentence, therefore, of the court is, that you be transported beyond the seas, for the term of seven years, to such place as his Majesty shall think fit."

So first of all, to the hulks went that incorrigible villain, Samuel Oliver, and there we lose sight of him. But he serves to draw our attention once again to the number of young boys herded together with men of whom, too often, they became the pupils in crime and vice. Thus in 1815, a year below rather than above the average, the hulks lodged one boy of 11 years old, two of 12, one of 13, four of 14, four of 15, and nine of 16. It was not until three years later that any suggestion was made of segregating them. Then Price, at that time Chaplain of the *Retribution*, wrote:

"I have heard it mentioned that it is in contemplation to erect Penitentiaries for juvenile depredators; but I am of an opinion, from the most serious deliberations on the subject, that it would be far better, and certainly would bear no proportion of expense, if a frigate were fitted up for their reception, instead of their being scattered as they now are through the different hulks and gaols. . . . In a ship of this kind, with proper overlookers (and everything would depend upon the choice of such persons), many of these poor children might be reclaimed. Let one part of the ship be allotted for their habitation, and other parts be appropriated for schools and places of instruction in different branches of trade. By being kept from all intercourse with adult prisoners, they would in a few years outgrow the recollection of their former haunts and companions; then, according to their general behaviour and improvement, let them be recommended to the Royal Mercy, previously taking care to seek out persons who will take them into their employ, as we do now every quarter with other prisoners; and as an inducement for their continuing in their situations with honesty, industry, and sobriety, let it be held out to them that for a certain number of years of settled *servitude*, Government will grant them a suitable reward. . . . Let it be remembered that they are at present but *children*, and so situated as to claim our sympathetic concern; by thus doing all we can for them, we are but following the direction of the wise man who declared that if we 'train up a child in the way he should go, when he is old he will not depart from it'."

The disposal of juvenile offenders soon became a favourite topic with Capper in his reports, and thus, we may judge, with the Home Secretary of that day, Lord Sidmouth—for Capper would scarcely have supported Price, had not the Chaplain's suggestion already found favour in high quarters. In 1823 the *Bellerophon* at Sheerness was set aside for juvenile use; about 320 boys were put on board her, and their spiritual guidance was entrusted to Edward Edwards—who very soon afterwards reported that "during Divine Service they generally conducted themselves with apparent attention; I strive to speak in a way to be understood by them, but being aware how hypocritically many even of them can demean themselves, I fear to speak in terms so strong as I could wish. . . . Within the half-year (now closing) 421 chapters of Holy Writ (averaging 20 verses) have been committed to memory and thence repeated in the chapel. Out of 318, 131 repeat the Church Catechism once a week. Out of the remaining 187 most, or the major part, cannot read."

Two years later the *Bellerophon* was broken up, and the boys were transferred to the much smaller 36-gun frigate *Euryalus*, stationed at Chatham.

Almost exactly twenty years previously, the *Euryalus* had been commanded by Nelson's friend, Captain the Hon. Harry Blackwood. When, in September 1805, Nelson had sailed from Spithead in the *Victory*, he was accompanied by the *Euryalus* and another frigate, the *Hydra*; when he joined the fleet off Cadiz, they were its only two frigates, and were employed largely in reconnoitring while the heavier vessels withdrew beyond the horizon in an attempt to entice the Allied fleet from the shelter of harbour. At last, after several ineffectual brushes, Blackwood was able to inform

Nelson on the night of the 20th October that the whole fleet was out and off Cape Trafalgar; whereupon Nelson approached, instructing Blackwood to keep in touch with the enemy throughout the night. At noon on the 21st, when Nelson attacked, the *Euryalus* was to port of the weather line.

The part played in the battle itself by so small a vessel was necessarily insignificant. But as soon as it was over, and the rumour of Nelson's death began to spread, Blackwood drew alongside the *Victory*, met Hardy, and learned from him the bitter truth. The two captains then went in the *Euryalus* to Lord Collingwood, the second-in-command, to convey to him Nelson's last instructions. Collingwood shifted his flag from the *Royal Sovereign*, which had been severely damaged in piercing the Allied line, to the *Euryalus*; and *Euryalus* took the *Royal Sovereign* in tow, in order to avoid the danger of shoals and a lee shore in a rising wind and a heavy swell. On the following day the *Neptune* became the flagship of the victorious but despondent fleet.

Had she now been used for the genuine reformation of young criminals, the last chapter of her history would have been even more glorious than earlier ones. But it will be recalled that Price, when he first suggested a frigate as a depôt for boys, had laid stress on the suitability of her Overseer. John Steadman was a man of mere routine, without insight into boyish minds, without any special interest in his job. From the first, the *Euryalus* was so crowded that no classification was attempted, and there were reproduced in miniature between her decks all the evils which half a century's experience elsewhere had not succeeded in entirely removing. When the number of boys on board rose to 383, Capper himself acknowledged the vessel too small for her work. Scurvy and ophthalmia broke out. The boys proved so refractory that open mutinies several times took place. And Price refused to conform to that official self-satisfaction which always put the best complexion on the worst facts.

"To effect something more than an external decency of behaviour", he wrote in 1827, "it is my most serious conviction that it is absolutely necessary not only that a plan of separation and classification should be adopted . . . but that these unfortunately neglected boys should be governed by persons competent to so highly important a charge; and in venturing to give this opinion I feel I am only discharging a duty I owe to the Government and the country. It is true that the exercise of power may restrain unruly dispositions, and the operation of sinister motives may produce a degree of obedience; but no permanent and radical reformation can ever be expected where the nature of mental and moral discipline is not understood, and as such, cannot possibly be adequately conducted."

And six months later: "I feel I am under the necessity of further pressing upon your notice the subject of my last report, in which I expressed it as my full conviction that no permanent reformation can be effected among the juvenile prisoners confined on board the *Euryalus* but by their being separated and classified . . . and besides, that a more efficient system than at present be adopted for the better ensuring the improvement of their morals and furthering the object the Government had in view in placing them here. The great importance of the subject will, I trust, be duly considered and meet the attention it deserves."

In these strictures our sympathies must be with Price; but Capper felt differently. "I regret to state", he reported, "that the Chaplain has not given that attention to the boys which I anticipated on his being appointed to the *Euryalus*,

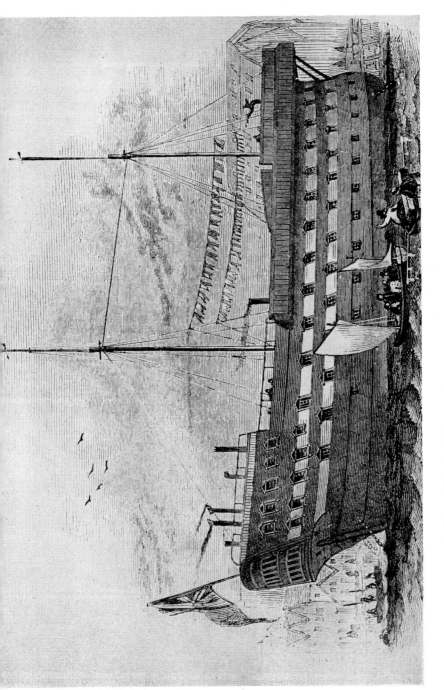

H.M.S. Warrior as a hulk at Woolwich, 1846

which he has attributed (most unwarrantably) to impediments which he has met with from the Overseer of that ship." With this disingenuous snub Price was transferred to the *Retribution* at Sheerness, whence he had come, his place being filled by the Rev. Henry John Dawes, who was sufficiently conversant with his job to waste no time in discovering imperfections. "It appears to me", he wrote after only a few months, "that the excellent discipline observed on board the *Euryalus* under the judicious directions of the Overseer, must in the end be productive of very beneficial results." A little later: "During the last three or four months there has been a very evident improvement in the behaviour of the boys confined in this hulk, especially in respect of their submissiveness to the officers set over them." And a little later still: "The behaviour of the boy convicts under my charge has been such during the last half year as to justify me in asserting that the disposition to amend, which I noticed in my last report, is increasing. In many of the weekly reports which are furnished me, not a single offence has been recorded; and whenever it has been necessary to use private admonition, it has been received, with one or two exceptions, in a becoming manner, and, I trust, not without benefit to the party admonished. The few boys in the hospital are very attentive to my instructions; and some of those who have died have manifested a feeling which showed that they were far from being insensible to the solemn truths or destitute of the consolations of religion."

To the Committee of 1835 he declared that he believed the boys to be reformed by the discipline on board—he had no means of knowing what became of them afterwards, but "can only judge by the improvement I have perceived in them while they remain here". In 1843 he reported that "such is the discipline kept up in the *Euryalus*, that I think so far from there being any danger of the more vicious corrupting the better disposed, there is good reason to hope that the influence of the latter is, in some degree, a valuable auxiliary in effecting that reformation which is one principal object in sending these unfortunate youths here".

Capper, on the other hand, seems to have been under no illusion that boys came out from the *Euryalus* much better than they went in. Time after time he dwells upon their "reluctance to learn or to apply themselves to their respective trades". "Eight out of ten that have been liberated", he told a parliamentary Committee in 1828, "have returned to their old courses"—and the degree to which such damaging admissions must have gone against the grain with him will be easily realised.

Everything on board seems to have combined to aggravate a determination to brutality and revenge upon the world. It appears possible, too, that the boys were canting little hypocrites. Under the tutelage of the Rev. H. J. Dawes would it not be difficult for them to be otherwise?—when, in addition to that gentleman's exhortations and admonitions, his youthful flock were compelled to listen to "an extemporaneous discourse, which generally occupies from fifty minutes to one hour"; and when "a blessing is asked before and thanks returned after each meal", although, according to a lad who had had experience of those meals, "you are half starved to death there". While as to bodily, as apart from spiritual, cleanliness, the boys were allowed to wash once a day in a cistern of salt water.

The day's time-table did not greatly differ from that in the hulks for men, except that for labour on shore was substituted tailoring in workshops on board; the boys were nearly all employed in making clothes for the Convict

Establishment, taught either by a guard or by an older convict. After midday dinner they were allowed one hour in the open air—but they might, of course, play no kind of game whatever. They walked like little old men round and round the deck, the slightest noise bringing a severe reprimand; so that, as Capper said, one would not know there was a boy in the neighbourhood. That was all the exercise those growing lads were officially permitted; with the result that, when animal spirits got the better of them, they were faced with the alternatives of bullying their weaker brothers, or of breaking some of the innumerable regulations and suffering in consequence.

Bullying appears to have been incessant. It was directed and encouraged by a set of boys who went by the title of Nobs, but was by no means confined to them. Thomas Dexter, the ex-convict who gave evidence before the Committee of 1835 and who, it will be recalled, had served as orderly in the boys' hospital, went so far as to say that in his opinion the majority dreaded the ill-treatment they received from their fellows more than the imprisonment itself. He had, he said, seen Nobs "take a brownstick and strike a boy over the arm, almost to break his arm, and the other dare not say a word to him". Again: "I have known it when three or four have been obliged to be locked up in a cell by themselves, in order to shelter them from murder—those they would call Noseys, that is, those whom they considered had been to the officers to tell them anything that was going on." And again: "I have known patients come into the hospital who have declared that they have not tasted meat for three weeks together, but that they have been obliged to give their portions to those Nobs, and that they have fed themselves upon gruel and the parings of potatoes."

In 1836 Dawes thought fit to draw Capper's attention

to the "great kindness" displayed by the Overseer towards his charges. A system of silence was then in vogue, and for long hours together boys were forbidden even to whisper. For serious infraction of rules the cat (up to eighteen lashes) could be, and was, administered, and for more venial offences the cane, with no limit on the number of strokes. But subtler punishments were found more effective. The following extract is taken from Capper's evidence before the Committee of 1832.

"To what discipline are the boys subjected in case of misbehaviour?—Locked up in cells or whipped with a birch.

"Is the whipping with the birch very frequent?—Not so frequent as you would suppose; we have not found it answer so well as locking up.

"They feel that more?—I think they do.

"Have they the means of conversing with their fellows when they are locked up?—Certainly not.

"Is it a dark cell?—It is not quite in darkness; we have a solitary cell for anyone who is incorrigible.

"You think solitary confinement a more efficient punishment for boys than whipping?—Yes, I do."

When we visualise this solitary confinement in a cell "not quite in darkness", we must remember that, still according to Capper, some of the boys were so young that "they can barely put on their clothes". The youngest boy on board at that time was only nine years of age "and deemed incorrigible".

Capper went on to defend the issue of "animal food" to them, although reminded by a member of the Committee that "the children of agricultural labourers scarcely ever taste animal food". What they were allowed, said Capper, was, after all, "very trifling"—it was only 7 ounces of meat a day to boys up to 15 years of age; and even that, it seems, they were lucky to receive, for the next time Capper gave evidence before a parliamentary Committee (in 1835) he revealed the fact that a cutting-off of rations "is more resorted to than any other mode" of punishment. "Stopping their meat and lowering their diet", said he, "has a great effect"—to which Steadman added that it was "a very good step for the first offence". Little wonder, perhaps, that the Nobs were eager to seize any food from their less hardy shipmates; but one is inclined to wonder exactly for what a blessing was asked before and thanks returned after each meal.

Another punishment was to prohibit offenders from seeing their friends. This, however, can scarcely have been regarded as severe, since, according to Capper, "in three months there are not half a dozen people come near them; they are nearly deserted". "Two thirds of them", he said at another time, "are either natural children or completely discarded." The Government very wisely tried to find friends for them to go to on liberation; when such friends were not forthcoming, it probably was, as Capper maintained, better to transport them at an early age to a land where they might eventually enjoy a fresh and healthy start in life than to turn them, alone and forlorn, into the tempting streets of a city, with nothing to look forward to and the memory of such a reformatory as the *Euryalus* rankling in their minds. Perhaps the kindest thing of all was to allow them to practise the art of self-mutilation, at which they were, at one time, adepts; for, on the word of Dexter, their treatment in the hospital ship was "remarkably correct". In hospital they did at least receive regular food and better accommodation, were free alike from Nobs and guards, and might even be treated with sympathy and humanity by such a man as that witness appears to have been. And so they resorted to all sorts of expedients to secure admission. A favourite one was to apply a red-hot copper button to their skin, rub the wound with soap, and then wrap it up until it turned septic and "piteous to behold". A much more drastic, though often used, method was described by Dexter.

"I have known several cases", he said, "in which they have broken their arms to get into hospital; they held their arms upon a form and let the edge of the table drop upon them and break them in two. They would get some other boys to do it for them, and then the excuse was that they had tumbled down a ladder."

For some years after about 1830 Capper urged more frequent transportation and at an earlier age than the 14 years then in vogue; gradually the numbers on board the *Euryalus* diminished, so that it was possible to foreshadow the abolition of the hulk (which had been confessed on all hands a failure) and the imprisonment of boys under 12 years of age in a special gaol on shore. At one time Dartmoor was mentioned, but the suggestion was allowed to drop, and that prison (which had been built for French captives during the Napoleonic wars) did not again come into use until 1850. Six years earlier, however, the *Euryalus* had been at last abolished, and an institution worse in some respects than Dotheboys Hall removed.

Chapter Seventeen

CRIME OR POLITICS?

THE three years between 1922 and 1925, during which a prison ship, the *Argenta*, lay in Belfast Lough for the reception of the Government's political opponents, were not the first in which hulks had sullied the waters of Ireland. Just a century previously, in 1826, two small vessels, the *Essex* and the *Surprise*, were established in the harbours of Kingstown (Dun Laoghaire) and Cork respectively, "to which all prisoners convicted and sentenced to transportation shall be transmitted with all practicable expedition". In a very short time they were crowded—and remained so throughout their period of service.

For more than thirty years, Ireland rejoiced in its own Convict Establishment, at the head of which stood Edward Trevor with the title of Medical Inspector and Superintendent of Convicts. He reported not to the House of Commons but to the Lord Lieutenant, and received the same salary as Capper. Among the returns of the Irish hulks are several described as being "required by J. H. Capper, Esq.", and once there is reference to a visit by Capper to Kingstown and Cork; but never does Capper mention Ireland in his reports, and it seems plain that the two Superintendents, though they were acquainted, had few direct official dealings with each other.

From the little we can gleam about Trevor, he does not appear to have been a man from whom Capper would have been likely to learn much good. Among the papers in the Public Record Office is a report, undated but probably written between 1835 and 1840, by Captain William John Williams, an English Inspector of Prisons, whom we shall meet again nearer home. His account of the conditions on board the *Essex* and *Surprise* is as lurid as almost anything we have learned concerning the English hulks in their unreformed day s.

"The hulks at Kingstown and Cork", he wrote, "are similarly fitted, and are nearly of the same size: they are arranged upon the very worst form of prison discipline although not the worst for security:—the upper deck is part fitted as a hospital, and before the mainmast as a mess or dining room: the lower deck as a sleeping room: the plan strikes one as precisely that which would be adopted for securing and lodging wild beasts; upon the upper deck they pass the day, lounging in idleness or basking in the sunshine, or when it rains in taking shelter under the awnings which project over the sides and walls of their airing yard: and at close of day they are mustered and passed into their sleeping room through a confined aperture, admitting the entrance of one at a time with difficulty, and thus rendering a rush outwards next to impossible—in this place they are locked up for the night. A glimmer of light is furnished to their apartment by a lamp placed behind an illuminator in both the fore and after bulkheads, and should disturbance take place during the night, these lights are instantly extinguished: but no one dares to venture into the prison."

His next paragraph deals more fully with the idleness to which he has already referred.

"There are no means of finding employment on board,

none of inciting the prisoners to habits of industry by uniform or routine occupation: none even of fatiguing the body, so as to diminish the activity of vicious minds by inducing sleep: no means of classification in separation, the youngest boy associating with the most hardened felon or murderer—there is an attempt at a school on board each ship, but it would appear that by far the greater part of a convict's time is passed in recounting his adventures in vice and infamy to his less wicked companions, and if this may be supposed to be particularly checked during the day by the presence of a Civil Guard overlooking the airing deck, it must be admitted that during the whole of the night their conversation is uncontrolled."

Strangely enough—since idleness begets sickness as well as sin—there was, according to Williams, "but little disease among the prisoners in either hulk"; so that "the hospital expenses are very low and the most judicious economy appears to have prevailed in the medical department, while the personal condition of the inmates of both hulks appears to present such a contrast to that of the lower classes of Irish generally that transportation upon the system now prevailing would seem to be the greatest boon that could be bestowed upon an Irish labourer".

Now Williams seems to assume that all the occupants of the *Essex* and the *Surprise* were felons brought to their present situation by law-breaking. That was certainly true of some. Felons they were in the sense that, in a time of famine, they had stolen sheep or cattle in order to keep body and soul together. It is noteworthy that, next to sheep-stealing and cattle-stealing, a very large number of prisoners were hulked for what were termed "insurrectionary offences"—in other words, they had been driven to dabble too deeply in extremist politics. But by far the greatest number had been put on board for reasons that were officially "not particularized". They were, in short, not criminals at all but political suspects, who, after a period at Kingstown or Cork, were transported to Bermuda, there to be clapped into a hulk with the most ruffianly of English criminals and given a diet which (miserable though it might be) was better than that to which they had been accustomed in their own famine-stricken land. The result of this treatment is described by John Mitchel, Editor of the seditious *United Irishman* and himself a prisoner (though a privileged one) at Bermuda in 1848. In his *Jail Journal* he sketches first the English hulk occupants as he saw and heard them, then the young Irish who were forced into sharing their company.

"But what enrages me more than all, is to think of the crowd of starved Irish, old and young, who have taken sheep or poultry to keep their perishing families alive in the famine, sent out to Bermuda to live in a style of comfort they never knew before even in their dreams, and to be initiated into mysteries and profound depths of corruption that their mother tongue has no name for. About two months before my arrival here, came out a great shipload of Irish—the harvest of the famine special commission—from twelve years of age up to sixty. They were all about three-quarters starved, and so miserably reduced by hunger and hardships that they have been dying off very fast by dysentery. As to the behaviour of these poor creatures, I learn from the commander that they have no vice in them, are neither turbulent nor dishonest, nor give any trouble at all. 'But', adds the commander, 'they will soon be as finished ruffians as the rest.' No doubt they will, poor fellows! He informs me that they were astonished, at first, at the luxuries provided for them . . . things they had never seen before, except in shops, and which they no more know how to use than Christopher Sly. Then they have liberty to write home as often as they like; and when they tell their half-starved friends how well a felon is fed, what can be more natural than that famished honesty should be tempted to put itself in the way of being sent to so plentiful a country?"

There appears no reason to dispute Mitchel's indignation. Bermuda was the worst of all hulk depôts, if for no other cause than that it lay farthest away from central authority. Yet the Governor of the islands, Captain Charles Eliott, was, on the whole, an enlightened man, and there exists a long correspondence between him and the Colonial Office over that very "shipload of Irish—the harvest of the famine special commission" to which Mitchel refers. There were, it appears, 704 prisoners in all; "many of them", he wrote to Earl Grey, the Colonial Secretary, "were convicted of stealing food and other agrarian offences; the first, no doubt, chiefly attributable to the dreadful calamity which befel the poorer classes of people during the last two years, and in the last degree to the inflammatory practices of others in the time of their desperate need. Perhaps her Majesty's Government may be pleased (taking all these circumstances into consideration, on the return of a state of comparative tranquillity in Ireland) to permit me to appoint a Commission in this colony, for selecting individuals from the Irish prisoners whom it may be permissible to recommend for removal to Australia on the ticket-of-leave or conditional pardon. These prisoners are, for the most part, friendless men in humble stations of life, and your Lordship will feel that they are entitled to any extenuating considerations which I can advise in their behalf, whilst they are conducting themselves steadily and submissively at this depôt."

Very shortly afterwards he returned to the attack in another despatch.

"I have the honour to transmit a list of 68 Irish prisoners

under 19 years of age . . . and I hope your Lordship will accede to my earnest wish that they should be removed as speedily as possible from a mode of punishment attended with serious risks and consequences not to be thought of without shame and grief. Poor and scanty food, and the hard things of their infancy, have for the most part left these lads with a lower stature and more childish appearance than their age alone would explain. Though it will shock her Majesty's Government to perceive that 12 of them are under 16 years of age, and that one, 13 years old, has been sentenced to 15 years' transportation for sheep-stealing! Sharp private whipping, as boys are usually corrected, and a brief season of separate confinement on short diet and hard work, under good guidance and instruction, would surely be a more appropriate punishment for these boys than transportation to the hulks. The reflection of their condition on release from such association and training is appalling, both for themselves and for society."

In due course the Commission was appointed, and some two hundred prisoners were shipped off to Australia. It is interesting to note that the *Bangalore*, the transport-ship in which they sailed, was detained in harbour for a couple of days; but although the prison doors on board were left open, Captain Eliott was able to report that "there had not been a single complaint", and that the Surgeon-super-intendent had "found the people orderly, clean, helpful and kind to each other, and intelligent in their ways". At the same time instructions were issued from Whitehall to the Lord Lieutenant of Ireland that no more Irish should be sent to Bermuda; but in later years other shiploads were transported, and after arrival there sometimes occurred inter-racial battles on board the various hulks. The most bloody of these began on the 1st June 1859 when the men were at labour and resulted in the death of one prisoner;

it was resumed that night between decks, another prisoner being killed and two dozen seriously wounded. The Rev. J. M. Guilding, Chaplain of the hulk on which the fight took place, wrote that "the spectacle on board the *Medway* hulk upon the 1st June last . . . would have appalled any humane heart. . . . Suffice it to say that a mere handful of warders was powerless to deal with the armed mob below decks. All that could be done was to fasten down the hatches, and when the work of butchery and carnage was over, descend below to fetch up the dead and wounded."

In the second of his despatches, it will be recalled, Captain Eliott drew attention to twelve boys under 16 years of age who had been sent to Bermuda. There were plenty in the *Essex* and *Surprise*, where they had come from. During eleven and a half years, the hulks in Irish waters had housed two boys under 10 years old; 118 between 10 and 14; 292 between 14 and 16; and 1847 between 16 and 20. During the same period, the total number of prisoners passing through the vessels was 10,763, of whom 9650 had been actually transported. Their idle time in Kingstown or Cork cannot have lasted long—yet long enough to grow weary of the irons from which they were never free; and long enough, probably, to taste some of the punishments— black hole, stocks, neck-yoke, or reduced diet—that were distributed by the officers with a lavish hand. And it was long enough, certainly, for them to conceive a bitter hatred for the British Government that was responsible both physically and morally for their situation.

Chapter Eighteen

BERMUDA

FAR away in the Atlantic, the Islands of Bermuda lie like a number of tiny specks of coral, limestone, and rich vegetation in an ocean of deep blue. Their climate is, in general, warm and moist; beauty and fertility are their birthright. Here it was, as we have seen, that convicts were sent to the station which, in spite of Captain Charles Eliott (who, as Governor, was also Superintendent of the Hulks), earned the reputation of being the most demoralising of any.

Demoralisation began, too often, on the voyage out; men sent from England were usually the most undisciplined and brutal of hulk occupants, and it was by no means always that the Surgeon-superintendents of the transport vessels were able to keep them in order. Mutinies were not uncommon. We hear of an occasion upon which the convicts took possession of two of the ship's guns, and were proceeding to load them when the pieces were recaptured. When, as not infrequently appears to have happened, they succeeded in making Bermuda too hot for them, and were, moreover, riddled with fever or half-blind with ophthalmia, they were returned as an extra punishment to the hulks in England, where they arrived again, mutinous and stubborn centres of disaffection. No more vicious circle could, one imagines, have been created; yet it was allowed to endure for nearly forty years.

It was in 1824 that the first hulk, the *Antelope*, was established in the Government dockyard on Ireland Island; in the next few years three others, the *Dromedary*, *Coromandel*, and *Weymouth*, joined her, the four lodging an average total of between 1200 and 1400 convicts. The *Weymouth* was abolished in 1836, partly because it had been intended to reduce the Bermudan establishment, partly because she could no longer be prevented from falling to pieces; another hulk, the *Medway*, took her place later, however, together with a hospital ship, the *Tenedos*. With the hulks, of course, went Chaplains, and with some of the Chaplains the customary rose-coloured spectacles. The Rev. Robert Mantach, for instance, comments gratifyingly on "the demand for the Scriptures among the prisoners"; the Rev. J. G. Murray declares that "every detail connected with this Establishment has been conducted in a manner characterised by the utmost quiet, regularity, and contentment"; while the Rev. J. Lough assures us that "the men appear perfectly happy and contented".

We have remarked that, in England, life in the hulks tended to produce tuberculosis. The warm, moist climate of Bermuda was the very worst that a tubercular man could be called upon to endure; doctors attached to the Bermudan hulks knew this, but raised no protest, did not even, it seems, take steps to insist upon the proper ventilation of the vessels. With the result that "in the close and stifling nights of summer", wrote the Rev. J. M. Guilding in 1859, "the heat between decks is so oppressive as to make the stench intolerable, and to cause the miserable inmates frequently to strip off every vestige of clothing and gasp at the portholes for a breath of air". Similarly, rations were ill adapted to the climate; periodical outbreaks of dysentery were responsible for many deaths, and scurvy (surely unwarrantable amid so much fertility) also took toll of the prisoners. In addition, ophthalmia, due to the glare of the sun on sea and limestone rocks, would cause men to stumble and fall as they walked even along a straight and smooth path. But the worst scourge which flayed Bermuda was West Indian yellow fever, carrying off hundreds of victims in the course of its many visitations.

During some years after the establishment of the hulks there, the islands were mercifully free; and when it appeared in 1829, it did so but slightly. It came again in severer form in 1837, 1843, 1844, and 1856; but the worst epidemic occurred in 1853, when 160 convicts lost their lives and a far greater number were permanently broken in health. July of that year had been unusually wet and August unusually hot; when introduced by a Spanish steamer from Cuba, where it was already raging, the fever swept like a tidal wave over the islands, persisting until the beginning of December, and claiming a total of more than 650 victims from civilians, military, and prisoners. The hulks themselves, grounded in thick mud, insufficiently ventilated, swarming with cockroaches and vermin, and housing a crowd of ill-fed and depressed men, formed excellent centres for its dissemination; and, moreover, panic appears to have taken place among those who ought to have been the first to battle against it.

One name, however, stands out from the inglorious throng—that of Price, an ex-guard on the Great Western Railway, who had been sentenced to the hulks for his part in a mail-bag robbery from a train of which he was in charge. He had been in Bermuda for about two years when the epidemic broke out, sweeping off convicts and officers alike. Throughout nearly the whole of three fearful months Price tended two stricken shiploads singlehanded. Small attention they can have received individually, of course, for the task was superhuman; but the moral example must have been of inestimable benefit, both to those who were already sick and to those who cowered before the threat of the disease. Price himself escaped even a day's illness; and one is glad to know that the authorities were sufficiently magnanimous to recognise his high devotion to duty. He was specially pardoned and sent back, a free man, to England.

When Mitchel was in the hulks at Bermuda there was one aspect of them which particularly infuriated him, although Mitchel himself could be (in theory at least) a stern disciplinarian. "I once asked the attendant who brings me my meals", he wrote in his *Jail Journal*, "what fault a man had committed who was flogged that morning. 'For giving cheek, sir', answered the man; which means, using insolent language; but when I hear the officers and guards speaking to *them* (as when walking on deck I often do), it is always in an imperious, insolent tone and manner, even in giving the commonest order; which might well exasperate sometimes the tamest drudge." A page or two later, he continues: "The language used by both officers and prisoners is altogether shipshape—damn, blast, or b—— your bloody eyes! One or other of these is the usual form of rebuke, expostulation, or encouragement (as the case may be) employed in the constant routine of duty. The chief mate . . . is a man high in authority and damns and blasts all the eyes in the ship at his pleasure, excepting mine and the commander's."

Howard, it will be recalled, had long ago protested against the "profaneness of the guards" at Woolwich; evidently matters had not mended in the intervening half century. But in those fifty years and more, the hulks had become an established institution, with all the authority of law and order behind them, hedged about with formality and tradition; in Mitchel's time the men, for their part, were compelled to behave in a manner undreamt-of in the more free-and-easy days of Howard and Duncan Campbell. They "have to take off their hats when they speak to the pettiest guard of the ship", and "dare not set foot on the quarter deck, even if they have an errand there, without uncovering and making low obeisance".

At the same time one appreciates the difficulties with which the officers were faced, put, as they were, in charge of some 1300 men acknowledged as desperate, and too far away from England to be able to make their urgent needs known to the authorities or to ensure the remedying of their just grievances. Nor did the Government at home always give them a ready ear; supplies were often indifferent in quality and late in arrival—in one instance, a delay of more than two years was experienced between the demand for and receipt of stores so vitally necessary as bedding and clothes. The Establishment appears to have been permanently understaffed, and the help of the military had far too frequently to be called for. But in spite of this, the guards did nothing to strengthen their authority when they treated prisoners with indignity and filth—still less when (and there appears to have been many) they took part in the illicit traffic between prisoners and native Bermudans.

This traffic was incessant, and so subtly organised that it required years of patient effort by the Superintendent to eradicate. Warders were constantly being dismissed for complicity in it, prisoners were constantly being transferred away from the islands. But still it continued almost unabated, a traffic in all sorts of forbidden articles, but principally in Jamaica rum. Time after time Capper in his reports called attention to the smuggling of rum on board. Once the men were under its influence, insubordination was

open and officers were attacked and maltreated—on board
the *Coromandel* in 1829 the mate was so violently assaulted
that he nearly died from his wounds. Tobacco also was
brought into the hulks in far larger quantities than were
permitted by the regulations; sugar, coffee, and a number
of other articles followed, to the profit partly of the guards,
more largely of the Bermudans. So deeply ingrained did
the habit of winking at this traffic become, that when steps
were at last taken to combat it, they were met with violent
opposition from guards as well as from convicts, on
the plea that it was to be regarded as "a recognised and
permitted practice".

Attempts at escape were frequent, though with slender
chance of success. The nearest mainland—the United States
—was some hundreds of miles distant; to reach it, a boat
would have to be better provisioned than a convict could
ensure by the hurried robbery of a house; nevertheless it
did very occasionally happen that a convict managed to get
clear away. His eventual hope lay in being picked up by a
foreign vessel willing to convey him to safety; but the mere
task of crossing the coral reef which surrounded the islands
proved too much for most would-be escapers, whose only
alternative was to lie hidden in the limestone caves or thick
woods, living as best they might, and then, when even the
most fantastic opportunity came their way, to seize it
greedily and trust in their luck. It was a favourite device,
when food ran short, to terrorise lonely householders with
threats of murder into leaving provisions outside their doors
at night. We hear of one ingenious, or fortunate, convict,
however, who was captured after six weeks in the cellar of
a provision merchant's shop, where he had been living on
the fat of the land. Another was once found dressed as a
woman; but a third, John Smith, known as Sydney Jack,
relied more on brute force than on his wits.

He had been concerned with four other men (one of them his brother) in the murder of a Berkshire clergyman about 1850, but, by turning King's Evidence, had managed to save his own skin and was transported to Sydney. Thence he escaped and reached England; soon afterwards he was re-captured and sent to Bermuda. At Bermuda he made two attempts; both were unsuccessful, and, in addition to being flogged, he was compelled to serve his full time instead of (as was usual) being sent home with some months of his sentence remitted. On the first occasion he seized a boat, provisioned it by robbing a house, crossed the reef, and was well on the way to the American coast when a change of wind blew him back. He was captured by a whaler, whose captain was deaf alike to his threats and his entreaties. Brought again to the hulk, he was loaded with irons, partly as punishment, partly to prevent a second attempt; but it was just while he was at this apparent disadvantage that the second attempt was made. He and several other prisoners similarly ironed were being marched to church by a warder when they secured their guard and ran into the forest. Sydney Jack determined at first to fend for himself. Knocking off his fetters, he spied a boat drawn up on the beach, and attempted to make away in her; but her ballast had been removed, and she capsized when he jumped in. He had no option, therefore, but to follow the rest; though they succeeded for some time in eluding pursuit, all four were eventually re-taken.

There was, too, an attempted escape from the *Coromandel* while Mitchel was lodged in the neighbouring *Dromedary*. Again the men managed to seize a boat; but she grounded on the reef and, after swimming ashore, they were compelled to take to the woods, where they were captured a day or two later, and sentenced to be flogged in each of the three hulks—a total of sixty lashes. "The Governor came this morning in person to Ireland Island, although it is Sunday", says Mitchel, "to give special orders about the mangling of these culprits tomorrow. It is to be a most solemn and terrific butchery. . . . Mr. Hire, the Governor's deputy, is highly important to-day; he always presides on such occasions and is said rather to like them."

Next day all the convicts were assembled to view the punishment, while a strong military guard, drawn up on the jetty near-by, covered the parade with their muskets. Mitchel continues:

"The laceration is finished. The gangs are sent out to their work after being mustered to witness the example: the troops who were drawn up on the pier have marched home to their barracks: quartermasters and guards have washed the blood-gouts from their arms and faces and arranged their dress again: the three torn carcasses have been carried down half-dead to the several hospital rooms. Though shut up in my cell all the time, I heard the horrid screams of one man plainly. After being lashed in the *Medway*, they had all been carried to this ship with blankets thrown over their bloody backs: the first of them, after receiving a dozen blows with miserable shrieks, grew weak and swooned; the scourging stopped for about ten minutes while the surgeon used means to revive him—and then he had the remainder of his allowance. He was then carried groaning out of this ship into the *Coromandel*, instantly stripped again, and cross-scarified with another twenty lashes. The two other men took their punishment throughout in silence—I heard one of them shout once fiercely to the quartermaster, 'Don't cut below the mark, damn you!' I have been walking up and down my cell gnawing my tongue."

There were, one suspects, more floggings, as well as a good many commendations, as the result of a big fire which broke out in the dockyard in 1855. Here most of the convicts showed themselves at their best; about a thousand of them, who had just returned from work, were let loose to fight the flames, and succeeded in confining them to the large warehouse in which they had started. But the fire was strongly suspected of being the work of incendiaries; and some of the prisoners took advantage of so unexpected an opportunity to indulge in wholesale looting, a few becoming hopelessly drunk in the process. Rumours also gained currency that a general rising was being hurriedly organised by the ostensible fire-fighters, and every available soldier in the garrison was called out to watch them with loaded muskets. But the conduct of the large majority was all that could have been hoped for.

It was not until 1862—five years after their abolition in England—that the Bermudan hulks were broken up; their continuance gave rise to a remarkable outburst by the Rev. J. M. Guilding, the most honest of the hulk Chaplains at that depôt. Writing in 1860, he says everything about them that ought to have been said by his colleagues since the first parson was appointed to the hulk service.

"Bermuda", he wrote, "is the solitary exception under the British Crown where these dens of infamy and pollution are permitted to exist. Both on the score of civilisation and humanity they have been everywhere else condemned. . . . If the hulks were so bad in principle that they have been totally abandoned in England, even with the careful supervision that the Home Government could bestow, what must they be in this distant colony, where abuses are more likely to grow up and far less likely to come to light? It is my painful conviction, after some years' experience of the matter, that the great majority of the prisoners confined in the hulks become incurably corrupted, and that they leave them, in most cases, more reckless and hardened in sin than they were upon reception. . . . Few are aware of the extent of suffering to which a prisoner is exposed on board the hulks, or of the horrible nature of the associations by which he is surrounded. There is no safety for life, no supervision over the bad, no protection to the good. . . . They are productive of sins of such foul impurity and unnatural crime.that one even shudders to mention them. . . . A mob law, and tyranny of the strong over the weak, exists below, which makes the well-disposed live in constant misery and terror."

To only one sentence, the first, can the smallest exception be taken; Bermuda was not the only hulk depôt then in service. In 1842 several hundred convicts had been sent to Gibraltar, to labour on the public works there. They appear to have lived for the most part in barracks on shore; but a hulk served as prison hospital until 1875—into the lifetime of a few people who are still with us.

Chapter Nineteen

THE GREAT EXPOSURE

BY 1847, so far as their employment was concerned, the hulks in England had, as it were, turned a complete somersault. No longer were they the home of those "daring and atrocious offenders" (now sent to Bermuda) for whom they had originally been brought into use; they were reserved for "all such convicts as from age, infirmity, or disease are not able to bear up against close imprisonment, those wholly unfit for colonial purposes, and such as require to be invigorated before they can be sent to their destination". They formed, in short, a large convict convalescent service, established partly at Woolwich, partly at Portsmouth (Chatham, Sheerness and Devonport had all ceased to be used as depôts), and lodging only about 1400 prisoners. At Woolwich lay the *Justitia*, the *Warrior*, the *Wye* for the reception of invalids, and an old French frigate, the *Unité*, as hospital ship; at Portsmouth and Gosport were the *Stirling Castle* and the *York*, with the *Briton* as attendant hospital. Capper still held the position of Superintendent, although all the work was done by his nephew, Robert, who was gradually, in accordance with the policy of the Government, reducing the number of convicts on board with a view rather to cutting down the expenses of the Establishment than to abolishing the hulks altogether.

At the beginning of March, Thomas Slingsby Duncombe, M.P. for Finsbury, made in the House a violent attack upon the hulks in general and, in particular, the treatment meted out to convicts by the Principal Medical Officer at Woolwich, Peter Bossy.

"It appeared", ran the report of his speech in *The Times*, "that the cruelty exercised was so excessive, the medical treatment was so brutal, and the manner in which the prisoners were treated when alive, as well as when dead, was such that it was utterly disgraceful to a civilised and Christian country"; and Duncombe went on to detail eight instances to justify his charges. All these instances were from the hulks at Woolwich, and all had passed through Bossy's hands. He concluded by demanding a committee of investigation.

Sir George Grey, the Home Secretary, called on Capper for a special report, warning him at the same time that an inquiry might follow. Now Duncombe had obtained most of his information from a convict named William Mawman Brown, who had been sentenced to twelve years' transportation for forgery. Brown had been employed at various times as clerk and as hospital orderly, and had thus enjoyed opportunities for seeing what went on in various departments of his floating prison. His notes to Duncombe were passed by a fellow-prisoner named Butler, while on the public works, to free labourers for delivery; others he managed to smuggle through himself; one or two appear to have been actually posted by guards. Brown was an intelligent, well-behaved prisoner, and on one occasion had successfully interposed to save the life of an officer who had been attacked by another convict. Yet in his report Capper did little but cast aspersions upon the character of the then unknown informer.

"To all persons", he wrote, "at all conversant with

prison discipline, and it is knowledge which is only acquired by long experience and careful observation, it is well known that there are always to be found among prisoners a certain number of discontented, ill-tempered men, sullen and disorderly, who cannot brook control and consider every act of compulsion, or attempt to enforce discipline of any kind, as ill-treatment, unwilling to work and who seek every possible means to avoid it. Of such prisoners the hulks were, of course, always liable to receive a fair proportion; but in 1843 the influx of prisoners to the hulks was suddenly arrested, and none of those remaining at that time in my custody have since been sent abroad; some have died; two or three only have been discharged by the expiration of their sentences, and the best and most well-conducted prisoners only have been liberated by pardon. All the men of worst character who were in confinement in 1843 still remain on board the hulks. Many of these, I am happy to say, who were originally riotous, disorderly characters, setting all order and discipline at defiance, have long since become respectful, peaceable, hard-working, trustworthy men; but all are not so. And it must not be forgotten that all the convicts sent to the hulks since 1843, until a few weeks ago, were only sent there because they were unfit to be sent anywhere else."

This failed to satisfy Sir George Grey; and shortly afterwards Captain William John Williams (whom we met as an Inspector of Prisons in Ireland) was called upon to conduct an inquiry "into the general treatment and conditions of convicts in the hulks at Woolwich". For the first time in the history of the Convict Establishment, prisoners still on board were allowed to give free evidence, without fear of consequences, and for two or more months Captain Williams' report was awaited with, probably, mixed feelings.

When at last it appeared, it was shattering. Though it
rebutted Duncombe in some of the corroborative details
he had put forward, on the general charge it vindicated him.
The state of affairs at Woolwich (and no doubt at Portsmouth too, although Portsmouth was not under investigation) was indeed "utterly disgraceful to a civilised and
Christian country". Yet the evidence was not more
sensational than had been offered to previous inquiries and
Parliamentary Committees; what makes Williams' report
significant is that it contained no attempt to minimise or
excuse existing defects on account of the system's alleged
"advantageousness'. It did something that had never been
done before—it looked facts in the face. Both it and
Duncombe's speech, to be sure, indicated an awakening
public conscience; the rapidity and thoroughness of that
awakening was in proportion, no doubt, to the complacency
that had preceded it.

A preliminary inspection of the little fleet at Woolwich
brought to light several faults which ought long ago to have
been remedied without need for official intervention. For
example:

"The ventilation of the ships, but particularly of the
Justitia and the hospital ship, is most defective. . . . The
water-closets without exception are most inconveniently
placed and imperfectly constructed; being unsupplied with
water, and having no vent to the exterior, the whole of the
effluvia passes into the classes between decks." The
system of lighting was also "very defective; and on board
the *Justitia* this defect has been endeavoured to be remedied
by allowing the convicts, in contravention of the regulations,
to purchase candles, it being impossible for them, from the
imperfect light from the lamps, to read or even to see
distinctly without." But such defects as these were small
compared with the "most disgraceful and discreditable"

state of filth in which Williams found the *Justitia* and the hospital ship, *Unité*.

In the *Unité*, "the great majority of the patients were infested with vermin, and their persons, in many instances, particularly their feet, were begrimed with dirt. No regular supply of body linen had been issued; so much so, that many of the men had been five weeks without a change; all record had been lost of the time when the blankets had been washed, and the number of sheets was so insufficient that the expedient had been resorted to of only changing a single sheet at a time for the sake of appearances. Neither towels nor combs were provided for the prisoners' use, and the unwholesome odour from the imperfect and neglected state of the water-closets was almost insupportable. On the admission of the new cases to the hospital, patients were directed to leave their beds and go into hammocks, and the new cases were turned into their vacated beds without changing the sheets. . . .

"The condition of the *Justitia* as regards cleanliness at the commencement of this inquiry, and for a long time previous, was no less discreditable than that of the hospital ship; there was a similar carelessness and neglect in supplying the convicts with the means of washing themselves; their blankets and bedding were dirty; they were insufficiently supplied with shirts and clothing; and their persons were loaded with dirt and infested with vermin. . . . Perhaps, Sir, I cannot place before you more satisfying confirmation of the discreditable condition of those ships at the commencement of this inquiry than in stating that it was found necessary to change the entire clothing and bedding of every convict on board the hospital ship, and that the supplies of new bedding, linen, and other necessaries, ordered for the establishment during the present and preceding month, very far exceed those of any previous period."

As to the laundries, "the linen and bedding of the convicts imprisoned on board the *Warrior* and the *Justitia* hulks is washed on shore, in small sheds, but the means afforded for the purpose are very inadequate, and the work is in many instances but very imperfectly done. The hospital bedding and linen is washed on board the hospital ship; a small and most inconveniently shaped cabin in the forecastle being appropriated for the purpose, for which it is wholly unsuited; the heat and stench were so insupportable at the time of my visiting it, as to compel me to quit the place." In recommending that all the washing should be done in specially planned and erected buildings on shore, he recommends also an adequate supply of baths for personal ablutions; "this being done", he comments, "I am persuaded that many of the just grounds of complaint which now exist of the unwholesome and almost insupportable stench prevailing between decks, whenever the prisoners are assembled there, would at least be partially removed."

Having noted that the omission of green vegetables from the dietary "appears extraordinary", and putting much of the blame for it on to Bossy's shoulders, Williams draws attention to "a very general spirit of dissatisfaction" which "prevails among the prisoners on board the hulks from Millbank and Pentonville prisons in regard to the oatmeal gruel (served out to them at breakfast) and a very lamentable waste is occasioned by the large quantities being thrown overboard from their positive rejection of it". Then follows the sentence: "They complain generally of its not agreeing with them; but I believe the real cause of their dissatisfaction to be that in the two prisons referred to the articles of food are of what may be termed a more luxurious description, cocoa being substituted for gruel and the bread being whiter and of finer quality."

Such a lack of suitable food and healthy cleanliness, he

indicates, amply accounts for the constant disease to which prisoners, who were already supposed to be weaklings, were liable—liable to such an extent that "the present accommodation is wholly insufficient for their treatment". For example, out of 600 prisoners examined for scurvy, 257—not far short of half—were found to be affected; and from the *Justitia* alone 157 patients were treated for ague in three months. But it was after their death that the greatest indignities were inflicted upon them. Says Williams:

"It is fully established in evidence that at night the dying convict has been left without the attendance of an officer, and at the complete mercy of a watchman, a prisoner selected from among the patients in hospital; that unless he expressed a wish, no minister of religion attends his last moments; that the breath of life has scarcely escaped his lips, when the bed on which he has lain is ransacked by his fellow prisoners, to find and possess themselves of any trifling articles he may have concealed; that the fact of his death is only announced through a skylight to a guard upon deck, and no further notice taken of it until morning; that the corpse is removed from the unscreened bed, laid upon the deck, and washed in the full sight of the patients; afterwards placed in a coffin, taken on shore to the Arsenal wharf in a boat, then placed in a wheelbarrow and wheeled round to the dead-house, and there deposited until taken away under the provisions of the Anatomy Act [which bestowed convicts' bodies on hospitals for dissection] or interred in the burial place in the marshes. In the latter case, the coffin, without pall or covering, is carried out early in the morning to the ground, and there left until the hour fixed by the chaplain for reading the burial service, when the steward of the ship, with six convicts, are present. The convict burial place in the marshes comprises a slip of unenclosed land, without any defined limits, and other spots in the vicinity were pointed out to me which had formerly been used for interments. I have every reason to believe it was never consecrated; and, considering the numerous and frequent burials which have taken place, it appeared to me singular that every trace of former graves was obliterated excepting those which had been buried but a few weeks."

It is only when we come to review the actual evidence on this point, however, that we appreciate Captain Williams' moderation of language. Robbery of the dead, it appears, was habitual, open, and vulturine; when a prisoner died, said one convict-witness, "they would almost fight to see if he had anything about the bed, so that they might take it, flannels or money"; another declared that he had seen corpses flung on to the floor to make certain that not the smallest trifle of his possessions should be overlooked. It was said that corpses "are then put into a hand cart, which is used to take dung out in, and carried to the Marshes to be buried. I have known bodies lying by the grave until the following day before the funeral service has been read by the chaplain." Sometimes, when post-mortem examinations were made, asserted others, it was not infrequent for parts of the dissected body to be left in pails in the shed for several days, open to view by anyone who might enter.

Inquests on prisoners were held in a public house at Woolwich, and no evidence was ever called from the convicts themselves; the coroner, J. C. Carttar, was in the habit of resting content with the testimony of Bossy alone. It was Bossy who, in effect, decided whether an inquest should be held at all, and he (or rather his pupils) who opened the bodies prior to post-mortem examinations—on which Williams comments acidly that "had the convict experienced any ill-treatment or neglect while in hospital, the Medical Officer would have been responsible therefor, and it is not very likely that he would incriminate himself in the character of a witness to his own acts."

Turning to the punishments inflicted on board, the regulations, Williams declares, "have been wholly disregarded". By one of them for instance, it was laid down "that in no case is moderate whipping to take place upon adult prisoners until the Superintendent is acquainted with the nature of the offence, and his approval to the punishment is obtained, and which in no case is to exceed 24 stripes. In order to evade this regulation, an untenable distinction has been created and sanctioned by the Superintendent, that flogging with a birch rod was not to be considered as coming under the category of whipping, and that to constitute the whipping requiring his previous sanction, it must be inflicted with a scourge. With this understanding convicts have always been whipped with a birch, without any reference to the Superintendent, and in one case a prisoner received 84 stripes. In several instances when the punishment was inflicted with a scourge, and admitted by the officers to be a whipping, the approval of the Superintendent was not sought for or obtained; indeed, on one occasion I observed a copy of the letter informing him of its having taken place. By the same regulation, the power of the Overseer to inflict solitary confinement is restricted to seven days, while the Offence Book of the *Justitia* shows cases of its being prolonged to 11, 14 [days], and, in one case, two months, in the cage of the hospital ship, the prisoner being kept in double irons and not permitted to take exercise."

The scourge, Williams mentions in passing—which had been employed, it will be borne in mind, upon the backs of men supposed to be semi-invalids—is "of unusual severity",

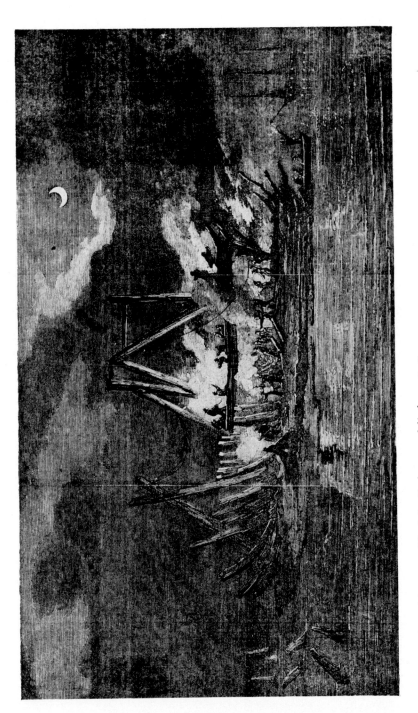

Convicts breaking up *York* hulk by torchlight, 1848

and he recommends "that fitter instruments be obtained, of a pattern to those in use at Millbank prison".

He comments, too, on the "very inaccurate and imperfect records of punishments" kept on board, and on the existence of a Minor Offences Book of which even Capper was not aware. In this book were apparently entered such punishments as depriving the convict of his dockyard pay, increasing the weight of his irons, or stopping his ration of meat. When pay was withheld, it "appears to have been laid out in bread and distributed, at the discretion of the officers, among those whom they termed deserving prisoners". As to the stoppage of the meat ration, it was in the *Warrior*, "without the sanction of the Overseer of the vessel . . . although the number [of its victims] amounted to from twelve to fourteen daily", and was so frequent that "one prisoner stated in evidence that he had been mulcted of 77 lbs of beef in three years".

Among those who were most soundly flogged were lunatics, whom Bossy, it will be recalled, would remove to asylums only if they proved violent or unmanageable. One of the cases cited in evidence was that of a prisoner named Kirby, whom the Overseer of the *Justitia* at that time (Henry Hatton) wanted to flog. Bossy expressed grave doubts as to the state of the man's mind, but the Overseer was adamant, and Kirby received his flogging—Bossy actually remaining to witness it, and Capper, when the punishment and Bossy's opinion were brought to his notice, passing over the whole incident in characteristically airy fashion. Several other examples of the Overseer ignoring the admonitions of the Medical Officer were adduced.

"Upon my first visit to the hospital ship", says Williams, "I found a violent lunatic, George Wilson, confined in what is not inaptly termed the cage. This cage is situated at the head of the ship, in the lower deck, is of irregular shape, having a frontage of about 14 feet by 3½ feet, and scarcely of sufficient height to admit a man to stand upright. The front is secured by open iron bars, and being elevated about 18 inches from the floor, the inmate is exposed to the full view of the patients. The place has been ordinarily resorted to for unmanageable insane prisoners and also on some occasions for prisoners under punishment, as in the case of James Venn, who was kept in it for two months. Taking into consideration the violence manifested by the prisoner George Wilson from the very first day of his reception at the hulks from Millbank, and the almost intolerable nuisance he was both day and night to the patients in the hospital and invalid ship for nearly three months, I think the Medical Officer ought to have taken the proper steps for his removal at an earlier period. There is also a singular omission of this man's case in the Surgeon's Journal, for although admitted to the invalid and hospital ship, and under the charge of the Medical Officer from the day of his reception from Millbank to his being sent to Bethlehem Hospital, there is no entry of his name or of the progress of his disease."

After remarking that "the inculcation of moral and religious knowledge to prisoners appears to have been a very minor consideration in the convict establishment, and regarded there more as a matter of routine than the most important element in penal treatment"; and having also drawn attention to the practice followed by nearly every hulk officer of employing convicts on private work, he deals at some length with Capper and Bossy.

"The infirmities of age and ill-health of Mr. J. H. Capper", he says, "have prevented me from obtaining from him personally explanations upon the many points in which he is involved in this inquiry." But he had submitted Robert to several examinations (from which the younger man had emerged in a crestfallen condition) and was in no doubt as to the part the Superintendent had played in the welter of slackness and petty corruption that was being steadily brought to light.

"In the absence of any direct supervision or control", he writes, "the officers of each ship appear to have acted independently of each other, each reporting individually to the Superintendent. The official intercourse has been carried on, in a very great degree, by verbal communications, made on the casual visits of the officers to the Home Office, of which no record exists, and of which, when required to be sustained by evidence, but very imperfect recollections remain. This carelessness prevailed even on the most important points of discipline. . . . The distance at which the Superintendent resided, combined with his feeble and imperfect exercise of the controlling power, and the want of system in the management, have been the obvious causes of the neglects and irregularities which have so generally prevailed."

As to the special report called for by the Home Secretary, in which Capper had begun by categorically denying every charge made by Duncombe and then tried to blacken the character of Mawman Brown, "it contains", says Williams, "many inaccurate statements; it appears to have been founded upon loose representations of facts; and his description of the convicts whom he supposes to have given information against the establishment, compared with those who have spoken in praise of it, manifested a spirit of unfairness and prejudice against the former. . . . Mr. Robert Capper in evidence states that he prepared the report and admits that its statements cannot be supported, and therefore any further notice of the subject may be spared."

Having disposed of the Cappers, uncle and nephew, Williams turns to Bossy.

"In no instance do I consider that either cruelty or harshness, in his medical treatment of the convicts, have been proved against him. His general conduct appears to have been kind, although in some instances, from anxiety to escape imposition, he may have imposed upon himself, in suspecting imposture where real disease existed, but the numerous simulations of disease to which medical men in charge of penal hospital establishments are subjected may well palliate solitary instances of errors in judgment, to which men in every condition of life are liable."

But having admitted so much, he proceeds to expose the actual state of the medical service.

Bossy, he says, "is a member of the College of Surgeons and a licentiate of the Apothecaries' Company, with a salary of £250. This gentleman, since his appointment of surgeon to the Convict Establishment, has purchased a business, and in conjunction with his brother enjoys a large private practice in Woolwich and its neighbourhood. His emoluments are further increased by taking apprentices, an advantage which he admits is ascribable to the office he holds, from its affording great facilities to the study of the medical profession."

Pausing a moment to point out the unfairness, to both Government and convicts, of this division of Bossy's attention between official duties and private interests, "it does not appear", comments Williams, "that any special authority or permission has been obtained by the Medical Officer for the admission of his apprentices as pupils in the hulks". They were employed in many ways to which he raises objection, and were even on rare occasions put in charge of the hospital; whereupon Williams remarks tartly that "I must observe, too, that the youthful appearance of these young gentlemen is very little impressive of confidence".

The Assistant Surgeon, Alexander Blyth, was "still in a state of pupillage", and spent the greater part of his time attending lectures at Guy's Hospital. However, "I should be doing a great injustice," declares Williams, "if I did not bear testimony to his unwearied attention to the sick, his kindness of manner, his devotion to his duties, and to the general confidence reposed in him by the convicts".

Among Bossy's administrative shortcomings Williams notes particularly the "loose and inaccurate" keeping of journals and registers, the improper power exercised in the hospital by certain convicts, the system, "carried to an extent almost amounting to absurdity" of appointing night nurses from among the sick themselves, and, most emphatically, the treatment of the dead, which, he declared, betrayed "such a disregard of common decency, upon a point where above all others the strictest observances might have been expected, that I cannot but consider the conduct of the officers as very reprehensible, and fully accounting for the feeling existing among the convicts". But although Bossy emerges with little credit, one is surprised not to see him receive an even more severe trouncing—cleanliness does not require great medical erudition to appreciate, and acquiescence in habitual filth and squalor in his own hospital ship is impossible to condone.

The report (of which, of course, only a few of the more important extracts can be given here), is completed by a comprehensive paragraph concerning the officers:

"Several of the officers employed in the Convict Establishment at Woolwich are manifestly incapable of performing their duties satisfactorily, in consequence of age and infirmity, others are so tainted by long habit with the vicious system of employing convicts in work for themselves, and other irregularities, and the evidence develops against other cases of such a suspicious character, that after giving the subject every consideration, I feel I can do no less than advise a thorough re-organisation of their whole body."

Such, then, was the immediate consequence of Duncombe's speech in the House of Commons; it must have startled that orator almost as much as it ought to have humiliated the Government—for Williams was, after all, a Government official who can have had no interest in representing matters as worse than they actually were. Sir George Grey was quick to declare that Duncombe deserved the thanks of the House for having drawn jttention to the state of the hulks—he had, however, only aust received the report and had not yet read it. But even when he had done so, he could not have foreseen to what upheavals it was going to lead.

For it was, at last, the beginning of the end.

Chapter Twenty

LIEUT-COL. SIR JOSHUA JEBB

NO time was lost after the inquiry of 1847 in making an effort to put the hulks in better order than ever before. Immediately after publication of the report, Capper, of course, was allowed to resign "in consequence of age and declining health", and was granted a pension of £240 a year. Robert Capper followed his uncle into retirement, with a pension of £130 a year. Bossy, on the other hand, was brusquely dealt with; in October he received a letter stating that a new Medical Officer "wholly unconnected with private practice, and whose time and attention will be exclusively devoted to the duties of his office" was to be appointed, and that "you will be relieved of the medical charge of the Establishment". At the same time the resignation of Dr. Geddes, Medical Officer at Portsmouth, was also accepted. To rid the hulks of these heads of the Old Gang actually cost the taxpayer more than £400 a year.

New regulations were drawn up by Captain Williams, and the whole Service was overhauled. The dietary was improved, the number of guards increased, supervision rendered more stringent, corporal punishment diminished, and an award for good conduct instituted. Taking the place of Capper, with the title of Manager of the Convict

Hulk Establishment, there was appointed Captain Herbert J. Voules, who (like the new Medical Officers) was "required to devote his whole time and attention to the duties of his office"; but after a year he gave place to the newly-formed Directors of Convict Prisons, under the chairmanship of Lieut-Col. (afterwards Major-General) Sir Joshua Jebb, whose intention it was from the first to abolish the hulks and lodge their inmates in prisons ashore.

Side by side with these attempts at rendering the last years of the hulks reputable went most inappropriate decisions. While gas was installed on board the *Warrior* at Woolwich, and the *Justitia* was abandoned on account of her age, the *Wye* and another small ship, the *Hebe*, were brought into active service for the lodging of prisoners. In them, convicts were never even roughly classified but were herded pell-mell as in the days of Duncan Campbell. It is true that these vessels were described as "temporary", but that did not make the evil less. Hammocks were slung close together (for the two little ships housed 400 prisoners) all through the crowded decks—which, it should be added, were less than six feet high; and since only one warder was on duty at night, there issued from those hammocks conversations precisely as corrupting as all that had taken place in similar circumstances since the first establishment of the hulks.

However hard Williams had tried, during the inquiry just concluded, to remedy the grievances of the convicts, it was very soon found that they were the first to object to the new and stricter discipline which followed. For several years they were in a condition of sullen insubordination; in certain vessels, notably the *York* at Gosport, a state of virtually open mutiny continued over a long period.

Late in 1847, the Chief Mate was attacked and severely

wounded; this was followed shortly afterwards by a serious affray, in the course of which another officer was attacked by a prisoner named James Impey. A new Overseer was appointed, in the hope that the introduction of different personalities would bring the prisoners to a reasonable frame of mind; disorders continued nevertheless, so that Voules at last requested the Home Secretary to sanction military assistance and the infliction of severer corporal punishment—both of which requests were refused.

The guards, new and old, also appear to have been unreliable—we hear of dismissals for drunkenness and neglect of duty, as well as a good deal of lenient superannuation. The number of successful escapes increased. Then, in June 1848, one of the guards, James O'Connor, was murdered in cold blood on the public works by a prisoner, William Attar; while just at the same time the Rev. R. Wright, Chaplain of Winchester gaol, formulated a strong complaint to the authorities in Whitehall against the "inefficient system of discipline pursued on board the *York* convict hulk at Gosport, and the commission of unnatural crimes by the prisoners". The Government, forced at last into action, held an inquiry under Captain Whitty (afterwards Governor of Portland Prison), as the result of which a number of prisoners was transferred, some to gaols on land, others to Gibraltar and Bermuda; guards were again dismissed, new ones taken on, and measures put into force to render work in the dockyard more severe and more closely supervised. Yet still disturbances continued, and in November it was suggested that a military guard should be stationed permanently on board—a step fortunately made unnecessary by the transfer of a big batch of ringleaders to solitary confinement at Millbank. Thenceforward all was quiet—until 1850, when fresh trouble broke out.

It began on that occasion in the *Stirling Castle*, but soon spread once more to the *York*; but, according to *The Times*, it was successfully quelled by measures which, though effective, seem scarcely to have been allowed for in the regulations.

"The émeute on board the *Stirling Castle* convict ship at Portsmouth", reported *The Times*, "was put an end to on Monday evening by the superintendent of the ship seizing up and flogging several of the ringleaders. . . . The émeute . . . which commenced on Friday, was followed by one on board the *York* on Monday, when the convicts refused to go to work, and commenced with the legs of their stools to batter the bulkheads and to use all sorts of abusive language to their keepers; but Mr. Barrow (we believe), an old army officer, who has charge of the ship, promptly seized two of the ringleaders; one of these men received two dozen lashes, and he then asked for a glass of water, which being given him, he told the officer he did not care and that they might flog away; his request was complied with and he was ordered to receive two dozen more, when he altered his tone and begged off. This prompt and decisive conduct on the part of the superintendent crushed the émeute in its bud."

All this time minor disturbances were taking place at Woolwich too, though they never reached the intensity of those at Portsmouth. On one occasion, a gang of prisoners determined to resist the removal of the wardsman of their class. Finding that the guards were about to remove him, says the *Daily News* of that time, "three of the most determined prisoners demolished a table that was in the cell and, arming themselves with the legs, dared the guards to interfere and remove Graham (the man referred to), who also threatened the guards and brandished a knife. The guards retreated from the cell, and as one of them, named

Frazer, was passing the bars, Graham struck at him through them with his knife, which touched the man's clothes as he drew back."

But it does not always appear to have been prisoners who precipitated disorder. Again according to the *Daily News*, "at the dinner hour on Friday a guard named Williams, who had received some provocation from a quartermaster named White, under the influence of his irritated feelings committed a violent assault upon the latter as he was ascending the brow of the ship. This was observed by all the prisoners, who were mustered outside the ship for afternoon labour, and the assault was immediately greeted by them with loud cheers."

Once more, in 1850, an "attempt at combined disorder" occurred on board the *Warrior*, and was subdued only by the removal of some twenty-five convicts, followed by a second large party, to solitary confinement on shore.

That the authorities could find no adequate method of dealing with these organised outbreaks is plain. They still further increased the number of guards, and swore them all in as constables; but in the end recourse had to be made to an expedient which had not been employed since the days of Duncan Campbell. Every hulk was supplied with carbines and cutlasses—an ironic comment upon the new and improved discipline which was to remedy the slackness and indulgence of Capper's reign. But none of the officers cared to face the responsibility of shooting down unarmed opponents, even though those opponents were themselves ready to do murder, should the chance arise.

In 1855 the first Penal Servitude Act was passed, substituting imprisonment with hard labour at home for long sentences of transportation; from the prisoners themselves it met with opposition so fierce that it culminated in the murder of an Assistant-Surgeon at Woolwich, and the stabbing of another officer. This time, however, opposition was quickly suppressed; and the last year of the hulks seems to have passed in comparative tranquillity.

It was at once recognised by Jebb and his fellow Directors of Convict Prisons that disorder and insubordination were due, not so much to the men, however recalcitrant, as fundamentally to the unfitness of the hulks themselves for the work they were supposed to perform. He therefore employed every means in his power to securing their abolition. But without wish to deprive him of credit for his performance, it should be plain that he was but the instrument of public opinion; Duncombe and Williams were perhaps its most effective awakeners, and Voules very well expressed the new spirit in the only report which he submitted to the Home Secretary, when he pointed out that "the hulks were altogether so ill adapted to the purpose, that I do not anticipate that it will be possible to establish any satisfactory system of discipline so long as prisoners are associated as at present . . . those who are well disposed are *led* or *driven* from their good resolutions, and very little hope of reformation or amendment can be entertained until means are provided of individual separation at night."

There were, however, die-hard Members of Parliament who clung to the shibboleth of "advantageousness". It was they whom Jebb first set about disillusioning. "The hulks", he wrote, "have not even the advantage of economy. On the contrary, experience enables us to say that they are expensive as well as unsuitable places for the confinement of convicts. The *Defence* hulk recently fitted at Portsmouth for the accommodation of 400 invalid convicts cost £8,960 9s 5d before she was fit to be occupied by prisoners; and the further annual cost of maintaining and keeping a hulk in repair, with other expenses, such as moorings, boats, etc., contingent on the use of vessels for this purpose, is much greater than on ordinary buildings."

He concluded the same report—the first for which he was responsible—with an explicit declaration of policy: "On reviewing the whole subject and the entire experience which has been gained concerning the occupation of the hulks, we cannot too strongly recommend that immediate measures be taken for abolishing them, and building convict prisons on shore, both at Portsmouth and Woolwich." And to the spirit as well as to the letter of that declaration he remained loyal; five years later, in 1854, he wrote again: "Our opinion of the disadvantages of the hulks as places of confinement for prisoners has been so strongly expressed in previous Annual Reports that we consider it here unnecessary to say more than that we consider those disadvantages radical and irremediable. . . . As a punishment and also as a means of reformation . . . we know none at all approaching in magnitude [of defect] to the association of the convicts in the prison hulks."

Meanwhile he stuck persistently to the "disadvantageousness" of the hulks—and events favoured him. The Governor (or Overseer) of the *Wye* and *Hebe* at Woolwich soon reported that those vessels were "totally unfit for the confinement of prisoners." A little while afterwards the *Warrior* was pronounced, in spite of extensive repairs, as "not likely to continue fit for use as a place of confinement for convicts for more than about two years". Three years later the Governor protested that she was "scarcely able to hold together . . . she is rotten and unsound from stem to stern"—tarpaulins had, in fact, to be hung over her leaking timbers to prevent the water from rendering her lower deck absolutely uninhabitable.

At the same time the apparent impossibility of trusting the guards, as well as the opportunities afforded to men on board to concoct future crimes, was emphasised by Sir Richard Mayne, head of the Metropolitan Police, before a Committee on Transportation in 1856.

"There is a case", he said, "at present in the hands of the police; the case of a very bad burglary, such as, I think, a few years ago we rarely had; it occurred at Stamford Hill in Middlesex. An old lady was tied in her bed, and her servants tied downstairs, and whatever was in the house was carried off. The police said they thought there had been very skilful hands concerned in it. The case occurred on the 26th April. Within about ten days, a warder of one of the hulks at Portsmouth and two other parties were arrested by the police, the warder charged with receiving the stolen property, the two other parties with being concerned in the commission of the crime. The offence of the warder was that he received a watch which was proved to have been stolen when the burglary was committed, and also other property, from two ticket-of-leave men who had been very shortly before released from confinement in the hulks. They had been released on the 30th March. They came to town immediately, lived in a very disreputable place in the Borough, and they are believed to have been concerned in the commission of this burglary very soon after. One of the ticket-of-leave men lodged with the warder up to the time that the police went down to apprehend the warder."

It is perhaps scarcely surprising to find the Chaplains trimming their sails to the new wind. Two typical examples may be quoted. The first is that of the Rev. George Livesay, at Portsmouth, who wrote:

"You will not be unprepared to find me express an opinion that I have long formed, that a hulk will never become a powerful engine of reform. Indiscriminate association, both by night and by day, and a want of proper means or space for an improved classification whereby the best disposed shall be secured from the pollution of the worst, convinces me that very little good can be expected to flow from the further continuance of the system." It would, he declared later, require "a more than ordinary pouring out of God's blessing" before "religious principles can be successfully inculcated and the hearts of the obedient turned to the wisdom of the just".

The second example is that of the Rev. Stewart Hanna, of Woolwich.

"I cannot blind my eyes", he wrote, "to the grave and painful fact that the hulks possess on the whole little of the character of a reformatory establishment. Of penal arrangements it is not my business to speak, and beyond the line of my proper office I have no wish to travel; but it is my plain duty not to be silent when I find inducements at work which, in my judgment, go far, very far indeed, to neutralise the benevolent efforts of the nation in the appointment of religious instructors, the gift of good books etc. to the convicts. . . . The remedy for this and other evils of a like kind is to be found in nothing short of the total breaking up of the present system of the hulks and the creation of a well-constructed prison on shore. Until this is done, there can be little hope of the Woolwich Convict Establishment accomplishing one at least of the great ends for which it was set on foot."

While Jebb and his allies were thus battering from various angles upon whatever remnant of public opinion might yet remain unawakened or sluggish, preparations were being rapidly pushed forward on shore for housing the prisoners who should, in due course, be removed from the abolished hulks. In 1852 the prison at Portsmouth was completed, and the two hulks there handed over to the Admiralty to be broken up, only the hospital ship *Briton* being retained in commission until she should come near to falling to pieces. Some of the convicts themselves were employed in demolishing the *York*, and one can imagine with what gusto they set about the complete destruction of their old and hated home—although it was winter, reported the Governor of the prison, "they frequently worked, at the first dawn of day, during the coldest weather, up to their knees in water. Not one of them had been ordered to work in this manner, but they had done so as volunteers and because they could thus work to better advantage."

The only hulks now remaining were the *Warrior* and the *Defence* (towed round from Portsmouth) at Woolwich, where the *Unité* still served as hospital ship. Suggestions were at first made that a prison should be built at Woolwich itself; no suitable site could be found and eventually Chatham was chosen, the prison being completed in 1856. To it all the able-bodied convicts were transferred, their transfer providing them with a welcome outing and the Governor with a pleasant surprise; for he reported that "I had them embarked on board a steamer for this place without any chains, no military guard, and I may say a mere dozen or so of officers to keep order. Before embarking the prisoners I addressed a few words to them, to the effect that I placed confidence in them and trusted they would prove themselves deserving of it. Nothing could exceed the praiseworthy and orderly conduct of the whole body."

On board the last of the hulks, the *Defence*, were left only those who were semi-invalid; their turn for a change of scene and discipline came more dramatically than that of the rest. On the 14th July 1857 this final relic of a three-quarters-of-a-century-old temporary expedient was destroyed by fire. Says *The Times*:

"At nine o'clock yesterday morning smoke was observed

issuing from the hold of the convict hulk *Defence*, moored off Woolwich Arsenal, which, on closer examination, was discovered to originate in the fore part of the ship, where about 200 or 300 tons of coal were housed for the use of the establishment. Every part of the huge vessel was soon filled with smoke, and the whole of the inmates were hastily removed to the invalid hulk lying alongside, called the *Unité*. Either from want of ventilation or some other cause, the entire body of fuel had become ignited, it is supposed, by spontaneous combustion caused by the confinement of gas. The united fire brigades maintained at the Royal Arsenal and the Dockyard . . . were promptly in attendance, and powerful efforts were made to extinguish the fire. It was not, however, extinguished for some hours. There is a probability of the fire having been occasioned by a spark from a pipe of one of the convicts picking oakum, although the regulations of the establishment strictly forbid the use of tobacco, which regulation, however, it is said, is relaxed in the case of certain invalids."

From the *Unité* the prisoners were first sent to the Invalid Prison at Lewes but later removed to a newly-built gaol at Woking, where they settled down permanently. Only the hulks at Bermuda and the hospital hulk at Gibraltar now survived quite cynically to spotlight the aspirations by which a felon might be morally reformed through imprisonment in what the deficiencies and perversities of human nature came, in fact, to make receptacles of woe.

BIBLIOGRAPHY

Abell, Francis: *Prisoners of War in Britain* (1914).

Annual Reports to the House of Commons: (British Museum, Accounts and Papers). Aaron Graham, J. H. Capper, Herbert J. Voules, Directors of Convict Prisons.

Barrington, George: *Voyage to New South Wales* (New York, no date).

du Cane, Sir Edmund: *Punishment and the Prevention of Crime* (1885).

Chevalier, Henri: *Un Corsaire de Calais, Tom Souville* (1895).

Colquhoun, Patrick: *The Police of the Metropolis* (1796).

Crooke, G. T. (edited): *The Newgate Calendar* (1926) (also Knapp and Baldwin's edition).

Dixon, W. Hepworth: *The London Prisons* (1850).

"Field Officer": *Bermuda: a Colony, a Fortress, and a Prison* (1857).

Garneray, Louis: *Les Voyages de Garneray* (1853); *Mes Pontons* (?1861).

Griffiths, Arthur G. F.: *Secrets of the Prison House* (1894); *Memorials of Millbank* (1875).

Hansard's Parliamentary Debates.

Howard, John: *State of the Prisons* (1777).

Ives, George: *History of Penal Methods* (1914).

Journal of the House of Commons.

Laird-Clowes, Sir William: *The Royal Navy* (1897–1903).

Mayhew, Henry (and John Binney): *The Criminal Prisons of London* (1862)

Middlesex County Council, Quarter Sessions Minute Books and other Records.

Mitchel, John: *Jail Journal* (1876).

Moore, Sir Alan: *Old Wooden Ships* 1800–1860 (1926).

Newspapers and Periodicals: *Times, London Chronicle, Public Advertiser, Morning Post, Morning Chronicle, Daily News, Scots Magazine, Sporting Magazine.*

Pike, L. O.: *History of Crime in England* (1876).

Public Record Office: Many papers under headings Admiralty, Transport Office, Home Office.

Reports of Inquiries and Select Committees of Parliament:
- 1778. Inquiry into the Act of 1776.
- 1779. Second Report of above.
- 1785. Lords' Committee on Transportation.
- 1798. 28th Report of the Select Committee on Finance.
- 1811. Select Committee on Penitentiary Houses.
- 1828. Select Committee on the Police of the Metropolis.
- 1832. Select Committee on Secondary Punishment.
- 1835. Select Committee of Lords on Gaols and Houses of Correction.
- 1837. Select Committee on Transportation.
- 1847. Inquiry into the General Treatment and Condition of the Convicts in the Hulks at Woolwich.
- 1856. Select Committees (Lords and Commons) on Transportation.

Semple-Lisle, Major J. C.: *Autobiography* (1799).

Vaux, James Hardy: *Memoirs* (1819).

Warung, Price (William Astley): *Tales of the Old Régime* (1897).

Waterhouse, Benjamin: *Journal of a Young Man of Massa-chusetts* (New York: Magazine of History, Extra No. 18, 1905).

Whateley, Richard, Archbishop of Dublin: *Thoughts on Secondary Punishment* (1832).

INDEX

A.B. (ex-convict), 113
Acts of Parliament, 3, 4, 9, 26, 193

Barrington, George (convict), 19–24
Beasley, Rueben (American agent), 76, 78
Beaudonin, Sergt-Major (prisoner of war), 81–83
Bermuda, 160–163, 164–173, 191, 199
Bonnefoux, Baron de (prisoner of war), 55, 57, 82
Bossy, Peter (Senior Medical Officer, Woolwich), 104, 141, 145, 175, 179, 181, 183, 184, 186–187, 189
Botham (convict), 109–112
Brett, William (convict), 116
Brown, William Mawman (convict), 175–176, 185

Campbell, Duncan, 3, 4, 9–16 pass., 27, 28, 36, 193
Capper, John Henry, 44, 90–97, 100, 107–108, 113–114, 137, 139, 140, 141, 148, 149, 150, 152, 153, 154, 155, 156, 157, 168, 174, 175–176, 182, 183, 184–185, 189
Capper, Robert, 95, 96, 97, 174, 184–185, 189
Chaplains (civil hulks), 9, 27, 30, 38, 40, 94, 103, 124–136, 163, 165, 172–173, 180, 184, 191, 196–197
Chatham, 46, 47, 50, 51, 53, 61, 71, 76, 78, 86, 100, 106, 116, 121, 135, 137, 143, 148, 174, 198
Colquhoun, Patrick, 18, 25, 31
Committees and Inquiries, parliamentary: Sir Charles Bunbury's (1778), 8–17, 27, 36; Transportation (1785), 18, 22; Finance (1798), 25, 26; Penitentiary Houses (1811), 39–44, 45, 92; Metropolitan Police (1828),

Committees and Inquiries—cont.
152; Secondary Punishment (1832), 107, 112–118; Gaols and Houses of Correction (1835), 119–124, 127, 151, 155; Inquiry into Hulks at Woolwich (1847), 174–188; Transportation (1856), 196
Cork, 157, 158

Deptford, 90, 119, 144
Devonport, 98, 128, 138, 174
Dexter, Thomas (ex-convict), 122–124, 155
Dignum, David Brown (convict), 21
Duncombe, Thomas Slingsby, M.P., 175, 177, 194
Dupin, Captain Charles (prisoner of war), 47

Eliot, Captain Charles (Governor of Bermuda), 161–163

Fontana, Dr. (prisoner of war), 83

Garneray, Louis (prisoner of war), 60–69, 81
Gibraltar, 173, 191, 199
Gillingham, 81
Gosport, see Portsmouth
Graham, Aaron, 36–44 pass., 92

Howard John, 2, 10, 12, 13, 14, 17, 25, 26, 28, 29, 30
Hulks (civil): Black Hole and cage, 6, 30, 154, 182, 183–184; boys in, 14, 31, 38, 123, 146–156, 160, 162, 163; cellular division, 30, 37, 44, 92–93, 102, 118, 120, 190; chapel in, 37, 93,